To Showing Up

To Showing Up

Raising a Glass to Lessons Learned in Everyday Life

KAYLA SMITH

RESOURCE *Publications* · Eugene, Oregon

Resource Publications
An Imprint of Wipf and Stock Publishers
199 W. 8th Ave., Suite 3
Eugene, OR 97401

www.wipfandstock.com

PAPERBACK ISBN: 979-8-3852-3045-7
HARDCOVER ISBN: 979-8-3852-3046-4
EBOOK ISBN: 979-8-3852-3047-1

VERSION NUMBER 110624

For Large, Hott Totties, Whitney, and all my Galentine's—I love showing up with you all.

For DG & Sayge—I hope my story shows you Jesus more than anything, and that you know how much He and I both love you.

For the miniBFFs—thanks for showing me the face of Jesus and His tenderness. LJ—we'll forever have the best day ever.

Contents

Acknowledgements

MOM AND DAD: THANK you for making my life possible. Literally. I am so grateful that I'm a part of our family and that I never have to wonder how much you love me.

Grandma Gerry: thank you for teaching me how to be generous in all circumstances, with whatever I have available. You are my favorite lady to watch Cardinals baseball with. Thank you for loving me enough to let me live with you during my Fun Fest summers, and for all those times you took Emily and I out for Chinese food when mom said no. You've taught me so much about joy regardless of circumstances, and I so love being your granddaughter.

Grandma Wilma: thank you for teaching me how to tell a story. You are my favorite lady to sit at a table with. Thank you for loving me enough to make me peach crisp when I come home, and for always reminding me of the strength I have because of Jesus. I love being your granddaughter.

Sister: thank you for keeping me humble and for having cute babies. Tell Michael I said thanks for the cute babies too.

Dr. Luke Bobo: I cannot thank you enough for making this book happen. You not only encouraged me to write this part of my story, but you helped me figure out how to live it all those years ago at Lindenwood University. Your presence in my life has influenced everyone I've come across since knowing you. You showed up to me when I didn't even know I needed it, and it formed me for the better. Thank you.

Lisa and Naomi: thank you for taking the time to read my words and fix some spots that needed fixing!

Katie at 4 Hands: thank you for pouring City Wide.

Jill: thank you for sitting with me as I continue to show up to God and myself.

Margaret, LeeAnn, Whitney, Leah, Emily, Tiffany, and so many more that I can't start listing or I'll never stop: thank you for living this life with me. For making it safe to show up. And for helping me become who I want to be, with God's help along the way. I love you all more than I can express. See you at Galentine's Day.

Introduction

To Showing Up.

It all started when I saw an Instagram post by Sophia Bush with the hashtag, #toshowingup.

The year was 2014 and I was deeply obsessed with Brooke Davis/Erin Lindsay/Beth. The level at which I creeped on her social media should be studied by scientists.

She would post photos of her life with the people she loved the most with #toshowingup tacked on at the end—an ode to, well, showing up. And I was influenced.

I started to consider what it meant for me to show up: to God, to myself, to my family and friends, to my church, to my dating life and singleness, to my body, to my pain. . .to everything.

I started showing up as best as I knew how and showing up began to change me. Turns out, showing up is simply the ministry of presence. The act of being there for someone, offering a non-judgmental atmosphere where stories can be shared, heard, and lived together.

So that's what I'm offering here. Stories of being heard, of life being shared, and how I am being formed in the process of it all simply by showing up.

Abbreviations

Eccl	Ecclesiastes
Gal	Galatians
Gen	Genesis
Hos	Hosea
Isa	Isaiah
Jas	James
Matt	Matthew
Prov	Proverbs
Ps	Psalms
Rom	Romans

1

To Life

"You can't just invite yourself over."

I heard these words more times than I care to recall throughout my childhood. Growing up I had the proclivity to do just that. Whether it was Tiffany's pool, the twin's trampoline, or Maggie's house to play POGs, I had no problem inserting myself into different spaces in life.

Turns out, showing up came naturally to me at an early age. I just wanted to hang around.

As a kid I would hop in my dad's truck on Saturday morning and ride to town listening to 105.3 FM KZNN the Country Superstation's Saturday morning oldies show. We would go to Town & Country, grab a donut (or donut holes depending on my mood) and an 8oz Dr. Pepper in a glass bottle, kicking off the weekend ahead of us. The oldies show on the radio offered my father an opportunity to grill me about my country music history. I love Patsy Cline, Loretta Lynn, and Charley Pride because of this.

Always wanting to answer correctly, I started to pay close attention any time the radio was on, Saturday morning or not. I learned the lyrics, the voices, the name of the songs, and even the featured artists when a classic duet hit the waves. I learned how to pay attention in an extended cab 1995 Chevy Silverado.

Paying attention is a big part of showing up. I have been learning how to show up my whole life.

The subsequent essays in these pages are all about showing up to life. They lay out, to the best of my ability, how showing up in these different pockets *of* my life have *made up* my life.

Showing up—being present—is one of the things I think I do best. Only recently have I come to realize that my life has been, and is being, formed into a life filled with the ministry of presence.

If you search "ministry of presence" on the search engine of our generation, you'll see ten pages of results pop up, most of which are articles written by popular Christian publications around the act of being present in other's grief and sorrow. Blog after blog reminds the reader that Jesus moves into places of grief and offers His presence to His co-heirs, and therefore we do too.

Obviously, we also see this reflected in the Bible:

> Carry one another's burdens; in this way you will fulfill the law of Christ.[1]

> Rejoice with those who rejoice; weep with those who weep.[2]

> For where two or three are gathered in my name, I am there among them.[3]

A devotional on ligonier.com says,

> The ministry of presence means that we will serve people even when it might make us uncomfortable. We will stand with people in the midst of anxiety and fear. Most importantly, in these difficult times we will be realists. We will not pretend things are better or worse than they actually are. We will address the situation appropriately, pointing people to the fact that Christ makes all things new.[4]

All of this is true and good.

And also.

The ministry of presence isn't just about others.

1. Gal 6:2 CSB
2. Rom 12:15 CSB
3. Matt 18:20 CSB
4. The Ministry of Presence, para. 4.

The ministry of presence isn't just about grief.

The ministry of presence is also about yourself.

The ministry of presence is also about celebration.

The ministry of presence is also about the ordinary.

The ministry of presence is also about Holy Spirit.

The ministry of presence is also about the physical world around us and the life we live in it.

As we show up to life, we offer ourselves to the world around us, and we open ourselves up to it. Showing up fully present is making the choice to be fully alive in that moment and to welcome the lives that exist around you. We *give* and *receive* beauty, grace, dignity, and love when we show up.

My life is full of the ministry of presence. Which shall henceforth simply be called "showing up."

Because that's what this whole book is about. Showing up. To love, to gyms, to swimsuits, and to friendship. Showing up and paying attention to how the presence of others, the presence of God, and my presence in the world has been forming me all along.

I grew up in a small town in the middle of nowhere south-central Missouri. The atmosphere offers a pace of life that is pretty even keeled, if I do say so myself. There wasn't much to do other than go to school, practice your sport, go home, eat dinner, sleep, then do it all again the next day. Occasionally you'd throw in some cruising around town and some bonfires by the river. I was fortunate enough to grow up in a space that allowed me to give my full attention to the day at hand.

As an adult, I now live in a world that does it's best to form me at a speedy, inattentive pace. If not tended to, my days consist of checklists to be checked, tasks to be tasked, and accomplishments to accomplish.

When I asked my dear friend Tiffany, a spiritual director by training and trade, what she had to say about the ministry of presence, she offered this thought:

> In the iconic 1986 movie, *Ferris Bueller's Day Off*, Ferris and his friends ditch class and responsibility to go experience delight and a little risk around the Chicago metro

area, all so they can consecrate being alive and 18. I love to think of the Ministry of Presence a little bit like that (only without the lying and stealing). Ferris closes the film saying, "Life moves pretty fast. If you don't stop and look around once in a while, you might miss it."

Ferris was on to something. What if we all gave our full attention, thoughts, and intentions to what was exactly in front of us? Whether it be our friend, our journal, our job, or our friend's dad's car we're about to steal?

That's what showing up is. Bringing all of our senses to the table, with the person or persons who share the same space we occupy. We allow our conversations to run tangents, our breathing to slow, our laughs to reach deep inside our bellies. We allow our bodies and our minds to sink deeply into the holiness of the moment, good and bad. We engage, and we offer dignity and attention.

And on that holy ground we are formed.

There's a story in the Bible about the prophet Elijah hanging out in a cave. He had just defeated the prophets of Baal in one of the most epic throw downs depicted in the Old Testament and was fleeing from Jezebel. While on the run, in a cave, he cried out to God, asking Him to show up. And in Old Testament epic fashion, a strong wind busted a mountain wide open, yet God wasn't there. Then, an earthquake, but God wasn't there. Next, a fire, and you guessed it, God wasn't there. But then, a still, small voice. A soft whisper. God was there. Not in the big, over the top, boisterous moments that Elijah was experiencing in his hideout, but in the tiny whispering of His presence.

That's what showing up is to me. Knowing that the big moments will come and will have an impact, but the holiness is often found in the whisper, in consciously being present to the moment at hand.

By intentionally practicing the art of showing up over the last decade, I've become convinced to the deepest part of who I am that this is the path to a flourishing and abundant life. Is it easy? Absolutely not. Is it worth it? Undeniably. It's awkward, and messy, and painful, and beautiful. I'll arm wrestle anyone that wants to disagree with me. Then I'll buy them a drink and convince them that I'm right.

Why is it the best path? Because it causes us to be whole. Not perfect, but fully who we are. It has the ability to take us to the depths of all that we are, individually and collectively.

By showing up with his five-year-old daughter on a Saturday morning, my dad taught me how to pay attention. Paying attention to the radio on a Saturday morning opened me up to paying attention to deer along the tree line in the field. To the perfume my friend wore every day senior year. To referees' names, and how much remembering them and saying hello during pregame mattered. To the way Starbucks smells on your clothes after you've been there for four hours writing a college paper. To a friend's red eyes and being able to ask what's wrong. To noticing how much a miniBFF loves word searches and blowing his mind with a surprise Amazon package.

Showing up *to* life and *in* life opens up our humanity. We're all afraid, on one level or another, of being known, yet that's all we really desire if we're honest with ourselves. Showing up time and time again offers the opportunity to create space for one another to be—known, loved, seen, heard, celebrated, held up.

I don't really have words for what it means to show up to my life, as the title of this chapter would suggest. What I have is a life full of the practice of showing up.

And my hope is that by telling my stories you will come to see that showing up is the best path forward, and a path that when walked together makes us more of who we really are.

2

To Love

I have lived my whole life fantasizing about my marriage. As a product of Disney and the peak RomCom era, I spent most of my classroom free time doodling Mrs. _____ all over my Trapper Keeper starting in 3rd grade. I remember swinging next to the boy I had a crush on in Mrs. Blankenship's classroom and thinking, "He'll tell our kids about this someday."

I haven't talked to that boy since 2007. But we do follow each other on Instagram, so I guess there's still a chance . . .

To this day, whenever I travel via airplane, I watch from my seat as people board and make (mostly awkward) eye contact with every male that turns the corner, assuming that will be our meet-cute and we'll live happily ever after. A practice I've leaned in to since I was 13.

Needless to say, I'm a fan of love stories. And of love.

My love story was going to go a little something like this:

- Begin seriously dating freshman year of high school—sophomore year at the latest.

- Go to college together. Engaged summer between junior and senior year. Married the fall after we graduate.

- Get good jobs, buy a home, have 3–4 babies by the time we're 30.

- Live happily ever after while raising athletic prodigies that will allow us to retire early.

When I graduated high school boyfriendless, I amended the above to be:

- Meet freshman year of college. Begin dating after sitting next to each other in AmHis201 and having the best of times laughing at how our professor pronounced Sacagawea.

- Engaged summer between junior and senior year. Married the fall after we graduate.

- See last 2 bullet points above.

College came and went. I did not meet my husband my freshman year. We did not sit next to each other in AmHis201. I was not married the fall after I graduated. As my timeline and pre-scripted love story continued to not play by my rules, I simply kept changing the story. The natural next option was to meet him at church. And it just so happened that I started going to a new church where there was an intriguing co-ed who decided to befriend me.

"This is it," I thought. "This is the beginning of our great love story."

He was single. He went to a Bible study. Basically, the whole package.

I did everything I could to put myself in his way—to let him know I was V interested. I said yes to every opportunity he offered to spend time together. Movie nights with other couples? Yep. Lunch after church and we ride together? Check. Happy hours and sometimes he pays but sometimes he doesn't? OKAY.

If he was asking the question, I was saying yes.

One of the yeses was for a study/homework night. We were not dating, but he thought it was a fun idea for us to share space and do homework together. We sat at a massive wooden table like we were in the library at Hogwarts, books spread across our respective sides, beverages of choice next to our computer screens, totally crushing the assignments in front of us. I was working on a paper about loyalty oaths in Missouri during the Civil War and yes, it was riveting.

At one point he got up to take a break and walked around the library for a few minutes. I immediately burst into tears. I was so overwhelmed with my feelings for this guy. How could such a good, God-fearing, delightful man want me in his life? When would he finally see that I had such deep feelings for him? When would he admit his feelings for me? How long, oh Lord, will You keep us apart?

And also, dang this is going to make for a killer love story to tell our children someday.

Spoiler alert: we did not get married, and we do not have children together.

My 20s continued with hit-and-miss crushes, short stints with online dating, and unfulfilled longings for a life that seemed out of reach.

I got really good and finding free communication weekends on match.com and spending as much time logged in as I could because I was too cheap to pay for a membership. One of the life hacks of someone working in the nonprofit industry.

Then, as another December rolled around with the promise of a new year was on the horizon, I decided to pay for one full year of online dating[1].

So that's what I did. I invested a chunk of change and committed to one full year of an online search for a husband. Eight months in and I saw a profile that piqued my interest.

Ginger. Guitar player. Christian.

We started talking and eventually set up a Date Zero[2].

---

1. If there's one thing I've learned in all my experience with online dating—apps, sites, you-name-it—it's that you must pay to play. These jokers on here for free are, 98% of the time, not quality.

2. I fully believe in Date Zeros, not first dates. Here is how Date Zeros work: you meet at a coffee shop/café/public space of choice for one hour. At the end of an hour, you leave. Works best if you have your reason for leaving ready to go before arriving. On this Date Zero my reason was a ticketed exhibit at the Art Museum. The other party doesn't need to know the rules because this isn't for them, it's for you. If you have a great Date Zero, you get to have a First

Anyway.

The Ginger and I had Date Zero.

After one hour had passed, I texted my friends and received replies of, "Yay!!!! I'm excited for you :)" and "Well that's definitely the most positive you've been after dates lately!!!"

Needless to say, we had a First Date. And then a second. And before I knew it, we were, what the kids would call, "dating."

Three weeks in I told him he was the only guy I was dating but I wasn't ready for the BF/GF label yet.

Three weeks after that—six weeks into the relationship—we were watching the ever-so-romantic *Shutter Island* at his apartment when he paused the movie, and the following conversation occurred:

Ginger: I have something that I want to tell you.

Kayla: (deep sigh) Don't say it if it's not true[3].

G: I . . . I love you . . .

K: (*tears running down her cheeks*) Okay. (*proceeds to make out with G*) Thank you. (*continues crying and making out*)

The next day I found a card at Target that said "I like you." on the front and, "Like, really like you." on the inside. I proceeded to fill the greeting card with sentences about how over-the-moon I was and how I wanted to get there—and believed I could—but that phrase was just too sacred to utter 6 weeks in for me.

He was everything I wanted: kind, observant, gentle, funny, loved movies and music and Jesus.

I told my best friends that I was pretty sure this was the guy I was going to marry.

Neither of them had met him yet.

The first few months of the-one-to-end-them-all romance were pure bliss. We ate, drank, made out, watched movies, went to Bible study, visited my parents, went to Christmas parties, basically did all of the obligatory fun things you do when you're dating someone in the fall -> winter months. My friends met him and

---

Date. If Date Zero is horrible, the only cost to you is one hour and (hopefully) a decent story for your friends.

3. I have really good foresight with some things.

gave me a thumbs up. Cautiously optimistic is a phrase I think we all threw around.

We posted our first Instagram photo together on Halloween night because I crush a good costume party. My friend's husband later told me that she ran into the room where he was to show him because we were all just that jacked about this relationship. All signs pointed forward.

Finally, after a couple of months and a lot of fantasizing over a Pinterest board, I told him I loved him. That sealed it for me. This was the guy. We would end up married.

My new love story went like this:

- Meet when I'm 29.

- Engaged after I turn 30.

- Married the following spring.

- Be married for 1 year before we start having babies.

- Live happily ever after while raising athletic prodigies that will allow us to retire early.

If there's one thing I should have learned by this point it's that I actually have no control over my own life. The only control I have is to open my hands to what the Lord has, or to close them and dismiss any gift He tries to give out.

It's a funny thing to long for romance, marriage, and a family for so long and then to have it within reach. Especially when you are the age your mom was when she was pregnant for the last time. I was 29, turning 30—an age that 14-year-old me thought she would be done having kids by.

I invited my 2 best friends to have access to my secret Pinterest wedding board and showed them the style of ring I would like to have. Just in case, ya know. Ginger and I continued in the ordinary day-to-day life of a dating couple, but I knew it was just a matter of time before we were engaged.

Then, around eight months in, something started to shift. I started to feel really stuck. We had passed the honeymoon phase of our relationship, and I was longing for things to go deeper than they were. I wanted this man to be curious about me—to desire to know every part of me he could before we got engaged and married. I would be so frustrated when he didn't ask anything beyond, "How was your day?"

I traveled to New York City by myself that year, and when I returned, I was surprised he didn't ask to pick me up from the airport. His complacency was confusing.

When I would bring it up and push him on it, the conversation was met with, "I don't know any better. I didn't have a good relationship to look up to growing up."

You can't ask someone to act on knowledge they don't have, but once you have that knowledge and you choose not to act, that's a whole 'nother podcast.

Shortly after my trip to NYC, a friend and I went to lunch and I word vomited my confusion and disappointment. She got an earful from a person that wanted to be married, wanted to be married to *this* man, but was starting to see how this man might not be it.

"As much as it could hurt, I'd rather see you deal with the hurt now than end up lonely inside a marriage with him."[4]

And as much as I wanted to give him the benefit of the doubt, I knew she was right.

I would spend the next six months holding out for a breakthrough with this guy. I wanted so badly for him to grab hold of the potential I knew he had.

He never did.

After a year and a few months together, we visited my parents at Christmas for the second time. I was standing in the kitchen with my mom, with my back to a window where I could see my boyfriend talking to my dad. G was talking with his hands while my dad was patiently listening. Then, dad reacted and stuck his hand out.

He and G shook.

I said, "Shit."

Loudly.

---

4. That is why friendship matters. She didn't cut him down or fill my head with what I wanted to hear. She told the truth out of love.

My mom thought something caught on fire.

I speed-walked to the bathroom where I promptly communicated to my friends what just happened and what my reaction was.

I knew in that moment I had to end it.

I had been showing up to love my whole life and I thought it was finally showing up to me. How could this thing that—just a few months ago I was convinced was the one to end it all—be ending at all?

I was so tired of trying to drag him along.

I was so tired of being single.

I was so tired of answering the question, "So, are you dating anybody?"

I wanted to marry him and move on.

But marrying him and moving on was the last thing I needed to do.

Could I have been married to him? Yes.

Could God have done good, redemptive things in our marriage? Yes.

Would my friends have had to endure a lot of hard conversations with a confused, hurt, and lonely wife to this man? Also, yes.

Four days later we went out to dinner.

As a fun source of false security and control[5], I like to place a lot of if/then situations in my life. The one I chose for that night was, "If he asks me how Christmas with my family went, then I won't break up with him."

Earlier that day I sat in my friend's bathroom while she cleaned and she asked, "So are you giving him another chance or is this it?" I replied with my if/then and said, "I'll be shocked if he asks so this is probably it." Remember my gift of foresight?

And it was.

He didn't ask. He wasn't curious. We ate in silence at a crowded bar. The lady sitting next to me commented on the pasta dish I had ordered. I had a better conversation with a total stranger that night than I did with the man that wanted to marry me.

---

5. Yes, this is sarcastic.

My heart sank because I knew I was going to break both of our hearts.

When you're dating in your 30s and the thing you want most is just within reach, the temptation is to look past the orange-red flags and just keep going along with it. The end is in sight. But in obedience, you can't have what you want just quite yet. It makes moving out of a dating relationship so, so hard.

We got back in his car and headed to my apartment. I timed out my conversation starter so we wouldn't have too much awkward silence left in the drive once the news hit the airwaves.

K: What did you ask my dad?

G: Well . . . (smirk on face) . . .THE question . . .

K: Do you really think we're ready for that?

G: Why do you think we aren't?

And therein lay the problem. Two people were showing up to the same relationship in two very different ways. One of us was in the harness, in the front of the wagon, pulling it along, while the other was content to just sit in the cart, enjoying the idyllic scenery along the way. My shoes were caked with mud, my hands were blistered, and my shoulders were tired. Until that night, he got by unscathed.

Now, I feel it important to own up to some things here—I was not without fault. There were plenty of nights where my friends asked both of us to hang out and I chose to exclude him. I had stopped saying "I love you" and didn't explain myself until he brought it up because it was clearly bothering him. I would get just tipsy enough to make out with him and then ask him to leave before things "went too far." I was not innocent in this downfall.

The tears started to flow as I looked out the passenger window, the red stoplight emitting the most appropriate glow.

K: I just can't do this anymore. I have been trying so hard to stick this out because I believe so deeply in the good that you possess. But I just can't. I am so tired.

G: (sighs heavily)

K: Does this relationship bring you joy?

G: Not always, no.

K: So we can admit that it's not good for either of us?

G: What does this mean? What are you actually saying?

K: (after what felt like half an hour of silence and shaking my head) I just can't be your girlfriend anymore.

He threw his head back against the driver's side headrest and I threw mine into my hands.

I got out of his car, went into my apartment, and texted my friends.

"He's devastated and I feel horrible about it. You could tell he was hopeful. I totally blindsided him and I feel terrible about it."

I was immediately met with, "Are you okay? What do you need? How can we help?"

"Can I come over and just process what happened?"

I received a Marco Polo response that was just an appropriately filled wine glass with the narration, "This will be waiting for you when you get here."

I was heartbroken.

He was heartbroken.

I totally blindsided this guy, and not Sandra Bullock style. But even in the aftermath of the ripping apart of a relationship I thought would lead to rings, and houses, and babies, and holidays, and traditions, I was still showing up to love. I was, and am, still showing up to what I believe is God's best for me.

I wasn't willing to settle for fine-enough.

I'm showing up to that "can't eat, can't sleep, reach for the stars, over the fence, World Series kind of stuff."[6] I mean, a girl's gotta have her standards.

And I'm not naive in thinking the "right" love will be easy. Have you ever watched a World Series? Those guys grind it out to emerge victorious.

But that's what I want. A teammate to grind it out with. Someone who will put in the work. Will get out of the wagon and pull it with me.

And in ending that relationship, I'm totally ready to show up to the next.

6. *It Takes Two*, 5:05 to 5:12

I started writing this chapter of my story on February 9, 2021. Little did I know that the spring/summer/fall to follow would be full of longing and unmet desire.

2021 was full of tears and desperation. On more than one occasion I sat on a friend's couch with streams of tears running down my face, saying through heartache, "I just feel so undesirable."

I had put myself out there with a guy I was convinced had feelings for me. He did not.

I signed up for dating apps and went on multiple Date Zeros with dudes that either 1) cared too much about their beer brewing hobby, or 2) couldn't carry on a conversation as far as they could carry a one-ton boulder.

I had resigned to this being my life—an endless stream of bad dates, good stories, and weekends full of my friends and their families. And I was okay with that.

I am not—I repeat, NOT—the girl that will say, "As soon as you're content, God will bring the right person along."

I despise, with a white-hot passion, flippant cliché sayings that give single people false hope, or make married people feel a little less discomfort when talking to us non-marrieds. If I am within earshot of one more person saying, "God is just making you into the perfect wife before He brings a husband along," I will burn things down.

Burn. Them. Down.

I am anything but content. I am far from being 'perfect wife' material.

But what I am is a woman that is totally obsessed with a man who is out of the wagon pulling the cart with me.

It's New Year's Eve 2021 and I'm in the eighth grade year of a relationship with a guy that pushes me, pulls me out of my comfort zone in the best of ways, sees the good in me and allows me to call out the good in him, and tells me how desirable I am anytime he gets a chance. We're maturing and growing, and I can't wait to see what freshman through senior year have for us.

Who knows. Maybe we'll live happily ever after while raising athletic prodigies that will allow us to retire early.

Here's the thing songwriter Cory Asbury is teaching me about stories—it isn't over if it isn't good, and if it is over, then it wasn't good. It is now December 2022 and I am officially 10 months out of the last relationship I wrote about.

One year ago, I was spending time with my boyfriend, sharing desires and goals for life, making dinner, watching movies, and planning on raising athletic prodigies that would allow us to retire early.

That relationship burned so hot and so fast. And I do mean burned.

It burned straight into the ground.

It was—to this day—the most painful relationship and breakup I've ever been through. Praise God for God. And for friends. And for mercy that is new every morning to meet me with love and kindness.

And, being nearly one year out, the thing I'm realizing as I read back through my words, showing up to love is not what I imagined.

In the same way that my love story didn't play out the way I thought it would in eighth grade, showing up to love is playing out differently than I thought it would 4 years ago.

Love itself looks nothing like high school Kayla thought it would.

Love looks like a text from a friend after she finds out that you've done some internet creeping in a moment of lonely weakness, finding out that your ex is engaged, leaving you to feel like you're the female Dane Cook from *Good Luck Chuck*:

L: Do you have plans tonight

K: No

L: Can you make some? lol

K: I really think I'm okay right now. I'm more sad about feeling like my life is stuck and everyone else's is going somewhere than I am about him, ya know

L:Don't let the lies win

That ain't true

You're literally writing a book

Shit be movin

And another:

M: A good luck chuck for ass hats maybe

Love shows up in many forms. And I'm showing up to love in hard, beautiful, productive ways. Showing up to love is no longer about showing up to date zeros, dating apps, or terrible boyfriends that do more harm than good. Showing up to love is about showing up to Love.

In a conversation with Nicodemus the Pharisee, Jesus explained to him his own purpose in showing up—to give of Himself out of ultimate Divine Love in order that the world might be saved through Him.

Showing up to love is about noticing the Divine in all aspects of life. Seeing that Love was present every time love has let me down. As I show up to a brewery on a Saturday morning, I bring Love with me. And when I notice Jesus and His divine Love in the present, the pressure of *this* love meeting all my needs falls away.

Showing up to love is more about meeting Jesus in every moment than it is about finding a husband and raising babies that will go pro in some sport that pays a lot of money. It doesn't diminish my desire to show up for love with a boyfriend/husband, but it does give me permission to show up to Perfect Love every day.

And honestly, is there any other type of love I'd rather show up for?

3

To Swimsuits

I grew up with a pool in my backyard. Not because we were rollin' in the cash, but mostly because we lived 30 minutes from the nearest public swimming pool and my mom liked to watch *Days of Our Lives* during the summer. She'd kick us out of the house and hang with Marlene Brady for a mid-day break.

A 24-foot above ground haven sat just off the patio and we definitely got our (parent's) money's worth.

When you have a pool, you have a lot of swimsuits. For a girl like me, shopping for and wearing swimsuits is fun for about no seconds. I hated it. The worst part of having a pool was deciding what to wear in it. I don't know if you know this, but swimsuits are tight and leave nothing to the imagination. They have a unique way of highlighting everything I have ever been insecure about.

But then something magical happened. At the beginning of my 8th grade year, Kate Bosworth starred in a thriller of a movie called *Blue Crush* and I learned about the magical world of rash guards. Almost immediately I ordered the exact blue and white Billabong surf shirt. That, paired with some board shorts, accomplished 2 things:

> 1—made me seem like I was the coolest, best dressed beach babe in Missouri, who definitely would be able to surf if she only had a board and some wax oh and also an ocean close by.

2—covered my body.

I was able to hide all that I was ashamed of under those clothes.

And that didn't just go for the rash guard. That was my wardrobe. Baggy, comfy, nothing hugging too closely. A lesson I learned early on was that my body was not my friend. It didn't look like any of my friends' bodies did. It didn't fit into the same "shirts" from Abercrombie & Fitch. More on that later.[1]

My body developed quicker, stopped getting taller sooner, and filled out in ways that made it clear I was to play the role of funny girl in the friend group.

So, I hid it. Not because my youth leader taught me that modest was hottest, but because I was ashamed of it. I couldn't fathom putting something on my body that would draw attention to it.

I don't know of many females who haven't, at some point in their lives, had a difficult relationship with their bodies.

Books have been written, podcasts have been recorded, Dove commercials have aired all in the name of reclaiming our bodies as beautiful, and I'm here for all of that.

But this is all about showing up.

Showing up to my body has been the most terrifying, yet freeing thing I've done in recent years.

Our bodies are weird. Have you ever eaten something then burped? Where did that even come from? Oh, my stomach acid? Why is there acid in my stomach?!

Scrape your knee, break a bone, pick at a pimple and somehow, it all goes back together, healed. Sure, it might take a cast and some Neutrogena, but ultimately it all goes back to the right place.

And if you're a woman, you've got the whole baby growing thing going for you. I've had the privilege of being around for multiple pregnancies with multiple friends and the process never ceases to amaze me. When a friend raises her shirt and points to an alien swimming from one side of her uterus to the other, my mind

---

1. Why did we put up with Abercrombie & Fitch and Hollister for so long? Just, why? Gen Z, please take our Millennial word for it and stop that right now.

goes to mush a little bit. I don't understand how someone can go through a pregnancy—either their own or with someone close to them—and not see how amazing bodies truly function and how incredibly designed they really are.

And yet, I've been afraid to show up to that beauty. I've been afraid of what it could mean for me to acknowledge that what God has created as Kayla Smith is actually good. That she is actually beautiful. That she has been named Beloved. That she is worth blessing.

I am not a person that exists well in my body. Have you ever seen *Futurama* where all the former president's heads are in jars? That's what I feel like. Always living just in my head.

But I reached a point in life where I just became so annoyed with being stuck. I was tired of feeling left behind in my own life. I was so in my head about so many things that I just wanted to move. So, I did. I literally started moving my body. I walked. I ran. I did workout videos on my phone that made me sorer than a person should be.

I started showing up to my own body.

And something started to change.

Sure, my body changed. But more importantly, my mind changed.

As my body started moving, I started feeling it for what it truly is—a carefully knit together vessel created to display the beauty and kindness of God to the world.

If you had the privilege of being involved in Christian culture in the 90s and early 2000s, you have undoubtedly been gifted something with Psalm 139:14 affixed to it. David, in penning a song about the all-knowing, ever-present God, gave women of my generation a rallying cry and tattooable text that we have clung to.

As I take a deeper look at the verses that make up the entirety of this psalm, what I read is a man recognizing and honoring the vast knowledge of a God who deeply loves him. The Lord knows our most inward parts. There is nowhere we can go to escape His presence. His creation has been intimately woven together, including the bodies that we live inside. And His thoughts about us are so precious and innumerable—we cannot comprehend how lovely we are to the Lord.

As my body began to move, my mind began to change, and I began to feel my body for what it truly is—a lovely, precious, and known creation knit together by a good and loving God—the natural next step was to buy a swimsuit. Or, more specifically, a sexy ass one piece (as dubbed by my dear friend).

Buying a swimsuit was almost like a baptism. An outward display of an inward change. A declaration of unashamed acceptance.

I wore that swimsuit just one time the summer I bought it, to my nephew's birthday party. A place where people who spent summers in that backyard pool would show up.

My parents no longer have that pool. Their children flew the coop and they wanted a fire pit. But our quaint little town now has its own public pool and that's where we had the party. That's where I got to make my sexy ass debut. And as my sister told me I looked good while we set up for the party, I let out a deep breath and knew that showing up in this way for myself was worth it.

There is great risk in showing up to a sexy ass one piece for me. And, as I show up, I realize I'm going to be okay. This body I've been given just might have more for me than I realize.

And I really want to be able to show up for her. Putting that swimsuit on kicked off the journey of me figuring out how to do just that.

4

To Gyms/Group Fitness Classes

At many points in my life, especially when asked to share my story in a group setting (what we'd call a 'testimony' back in my youth group days), I would say that the only two things I've known my whole life are sports and Jesus. I grew up in a household that went to church and the gym. Pews and softball diamonds. Fellowship halls and basketball courts. Sports and Jesus.

My parents met at a softball field. My sister and I both have pictures of ourselves around the age of 2 or 3 with a basketball in our hands.

Sports and Jesus.

My earliest memory of an athletic venue is of a gym in who-knows-where Missouri, falling asleep on the bleachers behind the bench where my mom was coaching her AAU girls basketball team. Peaches and Christy were on that team. And I'm pretty sure this is the same team where one teenage boy, who was there sup-porting his girlfriend, was playing with me on a concrete floor and inadvertently participated in the breaking of my collar bone. The only broken bone I've suffered to date!

Phil was my tee ball coach, and every time I see him he brings up my time on the diamond.

Coach Denbow invited me onto the court to play with the fourth graders when I was a measly third grade pipsqueak, and getting to dribble a basketball down the court for him was the most fun an elementary girl could've asked for.

Things really ramped up when Todd saw me playing shortstop for a city league team and invited me to play 12U fastpitch softball. I didn't know what love was until a bright yellow ball with a circumference of 12 inches came whirling at my face from 43 feet away, making contact with the sweet spot of my Louisville Slugger Lisa Fernandez signature model bat.

I started playing competitive softball with the Limited Edition Mustangs and never looked back.

I remember my body being strong. Even as a 10, 11, 12-year-old, I knew my body could crush it. Literally. I hit two home runs in one game! We won't talk about how those were the only two home runs of my 9-year career. . .

I was quick off the bag, could move so naturally when fielding a ball, and had a pure swing. I knew my body and knew it was capable of good things.

The thing about being an athlete is that you're expected to have an athletic body. To me, as a pre-teen who was just coming into her jock era, I had an athletic body. Athlete with a body = athletic body.

The thing about being a female is that you're expected to have a very certain type of body. And growing up in the late 90s/early 2000s, the body type of your dreams looked more like a 5'10" size negative zero with sticks for arms. Not a 4'11" (at the time) size eight with thighs that could crush doubles like it was their day job.

I started learning that I didn't have the right body around sixth grade. There's a very vivid memory of someone poking me in the stomach and making the Pillsbury Dough Boy laughing sound. That was indicator #1. More indicators started showing up as I realized I didn't feel comfortable in the same kinds of clothes that my friends wore. My group of friends and I went to Glick's to pick out matching shirts for school picture day. I wore that shirt one time— from the bathroom stall, to take my school picture, and back to the bathroom stall to put whatever t-shirt I had with me back on. You can see how uncomfortable I was in my shoulders with that orange and white shirt on. I preferred a one-piece swimsuit over a bikini[1].

When I started 'filling out' people started poking me. And challenging me to pizza eating contests, laughing when I would win, giving me the attention and affection I longed for from my peers.

Fast forward to high school where body is currency, I learned how to lean into self-deprecating humor, being sure to make the joke before anyone else could. I made friends by being the non-threatening chubby girl that would boost their ego, gossip about whoever they were gossiping about, and eat whatever they put in front of me because they "bet I really couldn't eat that too!"

As my body grew, I started to question whether it really was good. Sure, it could still do fun things on the softball field. It could take a charge on the basketball court. It could throw a discus far. But other than that, I didn't know if it was good.

And so, when my body wasn't on a field or a court, I started hiding it. Basketball shorts and oversized t-shirts became my standard. Not because they were comfortable (they are), but because they covered me. They made me feel safe.

In the early 2000s it was expected that you dress up for the first day of school. My senior year, I wore a basketball camp t-shirt and a pair of shorts, along with some kick-a all-white Nike Shox, and one of my coaches chuckled and said, "Of course. . ." when we passed in the hall.

Being an athlete kept me in the gym and working out. Whether it was the weight room, the court, or the field, I was moving my body with my teammates 6 days a week. I could keep up with them, I could lift as much—if not more—than them, and I could compete at high levels. My body and I were on the same page when it came to sports. We could hang.

College kicked off a new season. I was playing softball, working out twice a day with my team, eating in a college cafeteria (which in 2007 basically meant you didn't eat because it was

---

1. Again, we thank you, Blue Crush and Kate Bosworth, for the introduction to rash guards/swim shirts.

gross), and saw my body changing. I went on to play one season of college softball where I continued to be good with my body when we were on the field, where a coach was telling us what to do and how to do it and all we were responsible for was showing up and doing the thing.

Then I stopped playing softball.

No more sports.

Just Jesus.

And my body.

My body that I wasn't too sure about.

And Jesus that I was trying to figure out on my own for the first time.

I ended up leaving the softball team and spiraling into loneliness and depression. And food. I ignored my body. I ate food that wasn't good for it. I didn't move it in a healthy way. I did not treat my body like a good teammate in life, but rather just a thing that I carried around and didn't have respect for.

But again, the ideal body—the good body—wasn't my body. And I knew that. There was always a low-level hum of "you're too fat. . .undesirable. . .unlovable. . .lose some freaking weight. . ."

The other tricky thing about my body is that I've rarely had a man respect it. They've only used it for what they wanted. At 24, I was working through a pretty big heartbreak, finding out who my friends were and what Godly friendship looked like, and struggling with the 'fact' that no man could ever love me if I weighed what I weighed. I was going to the gym, working out at least three times a week, and still the girl that every guy saw as just-a-friend. I was *convinced* it was because I was overweight.

I was living in this world I created in my head that told me I have to operate like *The Biggest Loser*. That if I'm not losing 13–27 pounds a week, I'm not trying hard enough. I believed that this transformation of body, heart, and mind was going to be as easy as 3 hours in the gym every week. If a quick fix couldn't fix me, nothing could.

I would work out and eat well for a period of time, get on the scale, and see little to no change. Then I would go right back to the chips and cheese and pasta and guilt and shame and worthlessness that entrapped me to begin with.

And then I would try again. But my trying was always cloaked in shame. I still questioned whether or not my body was good. And when I went to the Club Fitness down the road, even with my friends, I was just going through the motions. I didn't want help. I didn't want anyone else to be part of the process. I wanted to do it alone, because that meant that no one else could judge—good or bad—the process. No one else could see my flaws. No one else could see how ashamed I was of myself. No one else could poke me in the belly and giggle like the Pillsbury Dough Boy.

At some point along the way, I resigned myself to this just being who I am. The overweight, funny friend who lived with deep insecurity and shame about the body she walked around in.

My shame really came to a head on a walk with Margaret in August 2019. She was telling me all about the gym she goes to, and while I admired her effort, I firmly proclaimed, "I will never go to a group fitness class. That is not for me. No thank you."

In the way she does, she smirked and asked why.

"Because I know what to do. Why would I pay to be in a group of people with someone else telling me what to do when I know what to do? There's no way I could work out with other people in the room! They would see me. They would see that I couldn't keep up. The vulnerability in that. . .nope. . .not for me."

"I mean. . .it's different there. You might like it. Who knows."

My resolved proclamation of "I will never" directed the conversation somewhere else that I can't recall.

A measly three months later I randomly asked if I could come over and do laundry on a Friday afternoon. "Of course! I will say, though, that I am going to a class at 4:30. You are so welcome to join me—first class is free—but no pressure. If you don't want to, you'll just be at the house by yourself for about an hour."

One thing I love about Large Marge is her gentle ability to invite me into things that are really uncomfortable and really hard, but really safe because she's there with me.

So, we went.

My never turned into an okay I'll try.

We went to a Ryde class on a Friday afternoon, and I cautiously loved it. The endorphins that pumped through my veins helped me feel like this might be a place I could fit in to. I didn't feel like everyone was staring at me. I felt strong. I felt like I could work hard and be met in the midst of the journey with kindness and care, not judgement and shame.

We walked out around 5:20 with the miniBFFs in tow, hoped into the Mazda, and firstborn and I sang *Hakuna Matta* because it truly is a wonderful phrase.

I told Margaret I liked it, and I would give another class a try, but I still wasn't sure I would join up full time.

The next week I went to another class. TRX this time.

The week after, I joined.

I was now (and currently am) a group fitness girlie.

But the story doesn't stop there. November 2019 to May 2020 saw my body go through the most significant change in my adult years. I lost a healthy amount of weight in the best way. I felt strong. I felt capable. I bought new jeans because I loved the way they looked, not because I felt weird about the way they fit. I bought a new swimsuit—the formerly mentioned sexy ass one piece, to be exact—and I actually wore it in front of people at a public pool.[2]

I remember going to the doctor for my annual physical in May 2020, seeing my weight on the scale, and for the first time in as long as I could remember, being delighted in the skin suit I wear around all the time. I sent a Marco Polo to my friend in tears, grateful to see my hard work finally paying off. My body—my teammate in this life—was back to being good.

Turns out, group fitness was transformative for me.

Not only did it help me externally change, internally it changed me too. I became alive inside my body. I paid attention to it. As a person who lives most of her life in her mind (Enneagram 6s stand upppppp!!!), moving my body in a bootcamp/circuit/TRX/ryde got me out of my head and into my physical self. I started to see

---

2. Don't worry about the 2020 of it all. It was a family birthday party in a small town and who even cares anymore.

improvement in my spiritual connection with God, my emotional connection with others, and my mental connection with myself. I was not just on a path to physical wellness, but whole-person health. I was becoming Kayla, fully.

When we look at the story of creation found in scripture, we see the story of a God who created things and blessed them all. He called them good.

> Then God surveyed everything He had made, savoring its beauty and appreciating its goodness.[3]
> One day the Eternal God scooped dirt out of the ground, sculpted it into the shape we call human, breathed the breath that gives life into the nostrils of the human, and the human became a living soul."[4]

The story of our faith kicks off with a good, creative God forming all things by the works of His hands and naming it *good.* This includes you and me. God breathed the *breath of life* into mankind. This, my friends, has been transformative in the way I view myself and my body. On my best days I'm able to remain in the truth that the Creator of all put His breath in my lungs. What greater physical blessing can we receive?!

And if we receive that blessing and open our hands to the gift that is the breath of life, the most honoring response in return is, "This body is good."

The gift of being a human that follows Jesus is that I can always come back to this truth. It may take a lot of work, and it may take a lot of time, but the truest truth is that I am good. The breath of life resides in me.

In the fall of 2021, I was at the peak of feeling good in my body and about my body. I started dating someone that made me feel like the most beautiful woman alive. He complimented me, cared for me, and always wanted to be physically near me.

---

3. Gen 1:31 The Voice
4. Gen 2:7 The Voice

I felt like this new and improved body I was in played a not-so-minor role in our connection. He was fit and strong and had a really nice butt.[5]

Group fitness got me into my body. Where I previously hid myself, I now let myself shine.

In Jr. High and High School, I was not a physically affectionate gal. I shied away from hugging my friends because, as a softball player that went to school with immature boys, I didn't want to be perceived as a lesbian, since that was already what others were calling me. Couple that with not feeling good about my body, I simply stayed away from physical contact with anyone.

But this new and improved Kayla with a boyfriend that couldn't keep his hands off of her. . .well she was very interested in (appropriate) physical contact.

Legs across his lap while we lay on the couch watching a movie? Yep.

Hold hands under the table while we're at dinner? Yep.

Kiss at a mini golf course in front of God and all His creation? For sure.

My body was finally getting me what I wanted: a man that wanted all of me.

Thank you, group fitness classes.

As time went on, my body became the most interesting part of our relationship. As an early 30s woman who was finally feeling safe in her skin, I allowed myself to honor my sexual, physical self. I have a history with viewing pornography, but I was no longer ashamed of that part of my story. I was no longer held by it. I wasn't afraid to feel, well, sexual.

I had learned what it meant to fully honor the body that God created and created good. I felt safe with God allowing me to learn what it meant to be a sexual being, a more whole person.

The first time he used my body for his own gain was on our official first date. It was the end of the night, we were in my car saying goodbye, and he grabbed my boob. Testing the waters. I pulled

---

5. I'm a butt girl and I won't apologize for it. God made me and God doesn't make mistakes.

back and told him that was off limits. He apologized, like all good manipulators do, and said he got carried away and it wouldn't happen again.

The next time was the night he officially asked me to be his girlfriend.

We had gone to a social outing with a bunch of my friends and, after meeting some of the crew, we went to his workplace for him to show me around. He took me to the back of the office, pushed me up against the wall, and took advantage of my body.

I occasionally wonder if he still has access to that security camera footage.

While I had been very clear about my physical boundaries—that I would not be sleeping with him—the topic of my body's role in our relationship quickly started to consume our time together.

I was a virgin, waiting to have sex with my husband. He had slept with girlfriends in the past and had a "high sex drive" so it would be a difficult journey but was wanting to honor God with his body and in our relationship. Or so he said.

In an effort to "care for me" he started offering massages. They started with him just working on my feet, legs, and arms, fully clothed and often ending in a make out session.

They quickly became full body, me laying naked on my couch.

While part of me was uncomfortable, another part thought it was okay. He was my boyfriend. He loved me. He was trying to care for my body.

My good body that I was also learning to care for.

So, I let him. I let him do what I believed he was doing—care for me.

But he wasn't. He wasn't caring for me or my body. He was taking care of himself. He "couldn't help" himself when his hormones took over and he was always sorry. Sorry enough to repent for a night and then do it all again next time.

He tried to get what he wanted one night toward the end of our relationship. We had been making out on my couch and had moved to the horizontal position. Glasses of alcohol had been consumed—something he made sure of every time we were at my apartment—and things were getting heated.

As things progressed externally, I began to regress internally. I lay there, eyes closed, arms crossed, tears starting to run down my face.

My body wasn't good anymore.

After what felt like eternity, but was probably closer to a few minutes, he finally noticed my scrunched up, tear-stained face, took a deep breath and said, "Are you crying?!"

His question was genuine. It wasn't angry or accusatory. He couldn't believe what he was doing, and I couldn't either.

And in that moment, I realized my body was part of the problem. He couldn't control himself when he was around it. So much so that he was using it for his own gratification, disregarding the person that lived inside of it.

It wasn't long after that incident that I finally got brave enough to confront him on his behavior and end the relationship.

Our last night together was terrible. It was emotionally draining and devastating. My body was kept safe on that night, but my spirit was crushed. The relationship that I thought would end the pattern of swipes to the left had ended.

The next day Margaret came over and, after recounting the events of the night before, I asked, "Have I been abused?"

"Yes," she simply stated.

I wept. I blamed him, mostly. I blamed my body, partly.

It was hard to breathe deeply from the breath of life that resided in me. I wasn't too sure where I could find that breath anymore.

Group fitness classes quickly became a form of punishment rather than care.

After my body's betrayal in my previous relationship, I used the boutique studio as a place to put my body in its place. One Saturday morning, Margaret walked into what would be my second class of the day, back-to-back in a room that is nearly 100* with what feels like 428% humidity. Noticing my sweaty disposition, she waved an invisible red flag, declaring her concern.

I did not treat my body kindly.

Over the next couple of years, I ignored my body, the good thing that has been blessed by the Creator since the beginning. I was still working out on a regular basis. One Monday morning I showed up to a 6:30am class at 6:25 and the instructor said she was concerned that I was going to miss because I'm usually there by 6:17. I didn't miss a day at the gym. But my body was back to just being an accessory to my life. Not a part of it. Showing up to group fitness classes was just another part of my calendar, not a formative practice in my life.

The composition of my body started to change in a not-so-positive (to me) way. Clothes stopped fitting the way I wanted them to. I was back to being the 15-year-old girl that felt ashamed to walk around in the skin she was given to live in.

And here I am today. 2024. I still go to the same gym. I still participate in the same group classes. I still (mostly) feel strong and capable. But my body is different. I have to fight to believe it is good.

It doesn't look the way I want it to look. It doesn't always move the way I want it to move. And it doesn't respond the way I think it should be responding.

Recently my spiritual director asked me who my favorite teammate in my sports life was. "Brandi Duncan," I emphatically and quickly responded.

"What made Brandi your favorite?"

"We were so in sync. We had so much fun. I knew what she was going to do before she did it, and vice versa. We enjoyed the game together."

"What could it look like for your body to be a teammate like Brandi?"

That's the fight right now. Not for my body to be a better teammate to me, but for me to be a better teammate to my body. For me to have fun with it the way I had fun with Brandi. To feel in sync to such a degree that nothing catches me off guard. To breathe deeply from the breath of Life that resides in my lungs.

I'm going to keep showing up to the gym. I'm going to keep showing up to group fitness classes. I haven't been to a Ryde with Maddie in a while, so that's on top of the priority list.

And the reason I'm going to show up is because I have known my body to be good. I have known it to be a good teammate. I have known us to be in sync with each other.

And I want that back. I want to be fully in my body and for both of us to be for the other's good.

What's interesting about showing back up to something you've known before is that hope is more tangible than it typically is. I know my body and I have what it takes. I know my "never" of group fitness classes is a far cry from who I am now. And I know that my friend Jesus is cheering me on, in the sweat room with me.

Showing up is as much about physical presence as anything.

And I want my physical self to show up, to be present and in the game, crushing doubles like it's her day job.

5

To Friends

I love my friends. And even though I might be a bit biased, I believe to the deepest part of my bones that I have the best ones.

In *Spiritual Disciplines Handbook*, Adele Ahlberg Calhoun writes,

> Friendliness doesn't require loyalties or major investments of time and energy. Friendliness may grease the wheels of human interaction, but it is not the same thing as friendship. Friends require a degree of intentionality and self-donating love that goes beyond friendliness and supporting each other in some act or enterprise. Friends know our being as well as our doing. Friends mutually and naturally supply support, sharing, counsel, fun, encouragement, growth, and a sense of being uniquely chosen and valued.[1]

For me, friendship is holy ground. And showing up to my friends is one of my life's greatest privileges.

The holiness of friendship is something I've had to work for. Growing up I mostly felt like the third wheel of all the friend groups. Finding where my presence fit was hard. The longing to be seen and known often led to me morphing into whatever group I was with at the time. You need me to gossip about the girl we're

---

1. Calhoun, *Spiritual Disciplines Handbook*, 175.

all mad at for no reason? On it. You need me to be the good youth group girl that has all the right answers ready to go? Done.

Looking back now I can see how adolescent Kayla was doing the best she could with what she had, and what she had was a deep desire for good friendship.

As I flew the coup and headed off to college, friendship seemed like it would be an easy endeavor. I was going to play softball for my university, so I had built in besties in my teammates. After a painful first semester of college, I had no besties and I no longer had teammates. I decided to stop playing the sport I loved, knowing that at the time it was the only source of social connection I had.

I can't tell you why the girl that would do toe-touches at half court before the last quarter of the boys' basketball game in high school had such a hard time connecting with people on her college campus. The only explanation I have is a mild identity crisis and some undiagnosed depression.

But I couldn't. I just could not make friends. And it wasn't because people were rude or off-putting or actively shunning me from all relational building opportunities. I just couldn't put myself out there. I stayed in my dorm room, tucked away from any sort of connection.

I did have a few friendly connections through a campus ministry I was a part of, but I didn't put effort in to allow myself to truly be known in those relationships.

Hiding was the path of least resistance, and it's the path I chose.

I think for some people, especially when you're young, stepping out, making a bid for connection, is too risky. It is a costly choice to risk connection. The idea that someone might turn away from me is harder to face than walking to class alone.

Long story long—college was lonely and hard.

I started going to a new church during the first semester of my fourth year of college. Your girl did a victory lap and ended up attending school for four and a half years.

In the fall of 2010, I found myself at a place that felt safe enough to begin risking connection. A group of people took me in and started showing me what it was like to show up in friendship. We would gather in back yards, at local coffee shops, and at the brewery on Main Street for Trailhead Mondays.

As they shared life with me, they invited me to share mine. This marked the beginning of me being willing to risk connection. Living in isolation had now become the costlier choice.

The funny thing about risking something like connection is the more you do it, the more you want to do it. I've found that regardless of how the risk plays out, I want to keep risking it, because you never know when it will pay off.

As I worked the muscle of risking connection, friendships started to fall into place. And the falling into place happened as I opened myself up to not only giving, but receiving, the self-donating love that deep friendship requires. Turns out, what I'd been searching for all along had a name: spiritual friendship. The kind of friendship that dares to show up and be seen in the presence of Christ and each other.

I didn't know it at the time, but showing up in this context would lead to the richest relationships I've ever known.

I had the benefit of my internship hiring Whitney as a new staff member, and she quickly became one of my dearest friends. She helped me come out of my shell and into myself at a vulnerable time in my life. I thank God, truly, for His provision in friendship with something as simple as someone else saying yes to a job opportunity. I was able to show up in that friendship because she did such a great job of showing up with me.

One of the biggest risks I took in showing up in friendship came with Hannah and Amanda. We found ourselves as part of the same group of friends at church that would show up in backyards and at Trailhead. We were all just weird enough to break off into our own little friend group. With an affectionate nickname featuring our initials, we shared all of our lives together. Not a week went by without spending time with one another. Countless group texts, tagged photos, and a weekend getaway to Chicago, I had found my spiritual friends.

When I think about showing up and risking connection in friendship, the first instance that comes to mind is a night with Hannah and Amanda at our local Starbucks where we sipped whatever latte was in front of us after women's bible study.

In college I had struggled with watching pornography and I held on to deep seeded shame surrounding my sexual brokenness. That night at Starbucks, I was past the depths of my addiction, but was in a place where I could sense the desire creeping back in. I had only ever confessed this part of my life to one other person, but only after she went first.

I was terrified of anyone knowing this gross part of my story. Especially in the evangelical circles I grew up in, porn was never a woman's problem. It belonged to the men. So, as a woman, if I struggled with looking at things on a screen, I had to keep it to myself. Women didn't deal with this. And since I did, there must be something deeply wrong with me.

At the encouragement of the one friend to tell others that I was living up-close life with, I sat down with Hannah and Amanda. "Hey. I have something I need to tell you guys. I have a history with porn. I haven't watched it in a long time, but I'm feeling like I want to. I don't want to keep this hidden anymore, especially because I don't want to fall into its trap again."

"I'm so sorry. What do you need?"

"How can we help you?"

"We love you and are here with you."

When I thought I would be met with shame and embarrassment, I was met with love and humility. I wasn't given a pamphlet filled with verses or asked how often I prayed about it; I was met with presence. For the first time in my life, I felt fully seen and safe in a friendship. I wasn't afraid to tip-toe around who I was and what I brought to the table.

Showing up fully, with my whole self and whole story, *and being received* in the presence of others allowed me to grow in bravery in every aspect of my life.

Friendship is a tricky thing. It's the only relationship with other humans that will last into eternity. And it's the only relationship with other humans that we aren't bound to by anything other than our word to keep showing up for each other.

Scripture is filled with nuggets of wisdom regarding the life-giving relationship of a friend:

> Two are better than one because they have a good reward for their efforts. For if either falls, his companion can lift him up; but pity the one who falls without another to lift him up.[2]

> The heart is delighted by the fragrance of oil and sweet perfumes, and in just the same way, the soul is sweetened by the wise counsel of a friend.[3]

> Live in true devotion to one another, loving each other as sisters and brothers. Be first to honor others by putting them first.[4]

Just to list a few. . .

I believe such high value is placed on the interconnectedness of friendship because, as God said in the beginning, it is not good for us humans to be alone. We are designed to connect with each other. For a lot of us (23% of church goers according to Table for One Ministries[5]) that connection comes through friendship.

Those friends showing up for me in my most vulnerable state laid the groundwork for how I do friendship to this day. The muscle of trust began to grow stronger that evening. Now, I only know showing up with my full self when it comes to friendship.

Another cornerstone moment in showing up in friendship took place at a camp that my job hosts every year for girls, grades 8 to 12. It was 2015 and we had invited our camp speaker from 2014 back to assist with breakout sessions. We thought she did a good

---

2. Eccl 4:9–10 CSB

3. Prov 27:9 The Voice

4. Rom 12:10 The Voice

5. "Americans are Single" https://tfoministries.org/single-adult-statistics -in-america

job, and we liked her vibe, so we asked her back. As a licensed professional counselor, she led a session on anxiety and stress. And as a staff person, I was simply placed in the room with her to be another adult presence. Between sessions we looked at each other and I said, "I think we should be friends."

"I think so too. But fair warning, I am terrible at follow up."

"Don't worry, I'm pretty good at it."

Two weeks later I texted her and set up a time to grab coffee.

A few months later we were reading a book together.

Not long after that she told me she was pregnant with her first child.

And now, I pick up her third child from preschool on Fridays.

What I have loved so much about this friendship is that all it is, quite literally, is showing up. It's not fancy. It's not full of big obligations or expectations. It is presence. And in being present with one another, deeply rooted familial connection has formed. My life has been formed in significant ways because we show up for each other.

Showing up with Margaret has helped me show up to myself and to others. The safety that our friendship has offered me has produced bravery and boldness I didn't know I had.

Some of that bravery and boldness came about on a Thursday night at Gospel Community group with my church. My GC has been a steadfast connection with people who love Jesus and are committed to seeing each other grow in the local church. We had a new, hot couple (she'll be uncomfortable reading that) join our group in the middle of the year. I was initially intimidated because they were so pretty, but she laughed at my jokes and he clicked with the bros, so easing into relationship was pretty seamless once I got over myself.

I can't tell you what the question was that prompted my response, but at some point I decided to bring up my past with pornography. I mentioned that it is difficult to talk about (even 6 years after my first confession to friends) because it's a man's problem, not a woman's.

The conversation in the room went on and the following day I received a text about getting together for lunch. "Some things you said really resonated with me and I'd love to talk some more."

We set up a time and had our first of many Mexican lunch dates. Her story is hers to tell, but the biggest point I'm trying to make is that if I wouldn't have shown up that Thursday night, I wouldn't have the friendship I have with her now.

Brené Brown says that vulnerability begets vulnerability. Sometimes all we need is for someone to go first.

Because someone else went first, I was able to show up. Because I was able to confess to my friends all those years ago, being met with grace, I was able to go first on that Thursday night. Because someone showed up for me, I was able to show up for her.

The flywheel effect of showing up is hard to stop once it's rolling.

I can't tell you how many baskets of chips and margaritas we have shared together while discussing the steadfast faithfulness of God in our lives. All because two people were willing to show up in friendship.

Showing up with each other has led to a tight-knit group chat titled Hott Totties & a Protestant[6], as well as me gaining a couple godsons. I'd probably have to write a whole other book to tell that story.

A gift of continually showing up with your friends is that they begin to know you and see you in ways you can't know and see yourself. Your blind spots are open to them, and when handled with love and care, they can speak into your life in ways that you can trust. Trust is the imprint left by experience, and my experience tells me I can trust the friendships I have built.

As a person who dates, I've also chosen to lay that part of my life wide open with my friends. They know when I go on dates. They have my location. They ask follow up questions when I don't freely offer the post-date information. I've been known to say that

---

6. I'm the Protestant. The other two are Catholic. And yes, the name originated on a night when hot toddies were consumed.

the "leave and cleave" part of marriage will be harder for me with my friends than my family.

You read earlier how a few years ago I was as close as I've ever gotten to leaving and cleaving. And without my friends, I would probably be in a difficult marriage right now.

The Thanksgiving before the world shut down, I returned home from a holiday break with my family. It was a Friday tradition to spend time with the aforementioned Margaret.

I drove back from my parents and went straight to my friend's house. I was 14 months into a relationship with a guy that I was pretty sure was headed toward marriage, yet something in my heart/mind/soul/body wasn't settled with marriage as the right next step. I got to my friend's house and, after typical post-Thanksgiving-with-family catch up convo, I asked, "Hey. Be honest with me. No b.s. Am I a better version of myself because I'm with the Ginger?"

Margaret, after pausing in the middle of chopping whatever was in front of her, took a breath, put down her knife, and said, "My gut is telling me one thing, and my head is reacting differently because I'm not sure if I can trust it. But the thing my gut is saying that I believe is true is no. You're not. You're not a better version of yourself because of the Ginger. You're a better version of yourself because of the way the Lord has been working in your life this year. Ginge has nothing to do with it."

I solemnly nodded and said, "Yeah, that's kinda what I thought."

The next day I went to Whitney's house because that's what I do, I show up to my friend's houses. Again, after the standard 30 minutes of friendship ramblings, I asked, "Am I a better version of myself because I'm with the Ginger?"

Whitney and Margaret are friends, but they aren't colluding with one another to sabotage my love life.

After a long pause, another deep breath, and a look in her eyes that greatly communicated deep-level friend love, Whitney said, "No. You're not. You're a better version of yourself because of what the Lord has been doing in your life, but I don't think he has anything to do with it."

Two people. One answer.

Two people who know me deeply, two people who have ached with me for the gift of marriage, two people that I have laughed more laughs with and cried more tears with, love me enough to tell me the truth. The deep breaths, the long pauses, and the love in their eyes told the story their words didn't—that they are undeniably on my team.

And sometimes being on my team means telling me what I don't *want* to hear but is exactly what I *need* to hear in that moment. This is the kind of friendship I truly want everyone in the world to experience and, at bare minimum, get a taste of.

Again, "The heart is delighted by the fragrance of oil and sweet perfumes, and in just the same way, the soul is sweetened by the wise counsel of a friend."—Proverbs 27:9 (The Voice)

When I think about the ways God puts skin on to show up in my life—these 2 ten-minute conversations are but a fraction of the way He does such a thing. I don't know how people make it without truth tellers like these in their lives.

Ephesians 4:29 (ESV) says, "Let no corrupting talk come out of your mouths, but only such as is good for building up, as fits the occasion, that it may give grace to those who hear."

My friends spoke grace to me when it would have been easier to fill my ears with pleasantries about how good this guy was and how I should just stick it out because marriage is what you want, right?

But that isn't the end game.

The end game is being like Jesus.

And that's what my friends push me toward every day.

Since 2013, under the tutelage of the great Leslie Knope, I've hosted a Galentine's Day celebration in honor of the spiritual friendship I'm privileged to hold so dearly in my life. What started as a nice dinner at local restaurants has morphed into an overnight extravaganza, filled with cheese and snack boards and wine and laughter. Stories shared, games played, lives intersecting for one night only with a group that I can't even believe I get to live life alongside. A conglomerate of all the tiny spaces I show up to, shoved together in a VRBO, tightening up the cord that is not easily broken. A foretaste of heaven, if you will.

Brené Brown writes in *Daring Greatly*, "The most powerful moments of our lives happen when we string together the small flickers of light created by courage, compassion, and connection and see them shine in the darkness of our struggles."

Friendship is the bulb. Galentine's Day is the electrical cord that connects them all together. Showing up to each other is the process of hanging those lights up on the porch.

And what a beautiful aesthetic those lights create in my life.

6

To Church & Faith

Let me start my saying I deeply love Jesus and I love the local church. I think, when done well—not perfectly, but well—the church is where people come to meet Jesus, to connect with the Saints, and to become more fully themselves than they ever have been.

Let me also recognize that a lot of people have been hurt by the church. Including me. I believe too much weight has been put on the church to be the end-all-be-all for followers of Jesus. For some, I think church has replaced God.

But for me, I love showing up to church.

I started going to church when I was in utero. My parents were married in the same church I was baptized in. This also happens to be the same church that my ancestors founded in 1854. I'm a 7th generation churchgoer.

A tiny country church that's been around since before the Civil War, along the side of a rural highway with a cemetery on one side and a parsonage on the other, Boone Creek Baptist is a building that I could still walk through with my eyes closed.

Showing up to church as a kid meant fighting my mom about what clothes I was going to wear. She always won out and I never got to wear basketball shorts on a Sunday morning.

Sunday School at 10am, morning service at 11, dinner at Grandma's house right after. That was the Sunday routine. I would show up to Sunday School with Amber, JK, Nikki, Ashley, and Brandon where we would learn all about the stories of our faith. About how Noah listened and obeyed. Abraham had faith that God would provide. David stepped out in God's strength and defeated the giant.

We learned about Jesus' great love for us, and I, personally, saw that love reflected on the teachers that brought out their best on Sunday mornings for these 7-year-olds that were more interested in going outside to play than sitting in a paneled room with coloring sheets.

As I grew up and changed, showing up to church didn't. Sunday School at 10am, morning service at 11, dinner at Grandma's house right after. There was never a question about where the Smiths would be on a Sunday morning.

That's if we were in town.

There were about 8 summers where we spent our Sundays on a softball diamond, but other than that. . .

I loved going to church. I loved talking about faith with my friends. I loved sitting in the front row, listening to Bro. Jimmy preach and taking notes in a journal I still have tucked away somewhere. I loved listening to Connie lead us in worship and challenging us to raise a joyful noise unto the Lord. I loved it.

Also, I didn't have much of a choice of whether or not I showed up while I lived with my parents. 7th generation churchgoer and all.

A really cute thing a lot of people in my generation have done (or are doing) is this tiny little thing called deconstruction.

According to Joe Terrell, "Christian deconstruction is the process by which a Christian critically reevaluates the tenets and doctrines of traditional Christianity and emerges with a different perspective on their faith."[1]

Terrell also notes that in his book *When Everything Catches Fire*, Brian Zahnd says that deconstruction is, "a crisis of Christian

---

1. Terrell, "Five Real Reasons Young People Are Deconstructing Christianity," para. 5.

faith that leads to either a reevaluation of Christianity or sometimes a total abandonment of Christianity."[2]

This does not mean that everyone who deconstructs their faith leaves their faith. That would be deconversion.

But the loudest voices on my TikTok FYP would suggest that most deconstruction has led to deconversion.

Might I suggest it's because we don't know how to show up to church? In the midst of not knowing how to show up to church we've also lost what it means to show up to our faith.

Carey Nieuwhof writes that there are five real reasons young people—Millennials like me included—have stopped showing up to church:

1. Irrelevance, Hypocrisy, and Moral Failure

2. God Is Missing in the Church

3. Legitimate Doubt Is Prohibited

4. They're not Learning About God

5. They're not Finding Community[3]

In my humble, 7th generation church-goer opinion . . .

We've traded fellowship for fog machines.

We've traded sharing in meals for sharing in social media posts.

We've traded prayer for platforms.

I think we've traded our trust in Jesus as the true King of the Kingdom for a belief that without us, the Kingdom would fall.

I, myself, have gone through a deconstruction of my Christian faith.

I started seeing a Spiritual Director in the fall of 2020 because I knew something was stuck. Eight months into my first global pandemic, I was feeling surprisingly good about a lot of things, but

2. Terrell, "Five Real Reasons Young People Are Deconstructing Christianity," para. 6.

3. Nieuwhof, "5 Reasons People Have Stopped Attending Your Church (Especially Millennials).

knew I needed some outside presence to sit with me for a while. And that led to Spiritual Direction.

Spiritual Direction is a relationship between a trained spiritual guide and someone (me) who wants to deepen their relationship with God. I spend one hour every month just talking about the journey of my life with Jesus.

I was going to church—showing up to host our fully livestreamed services—every week, reading my Bible, present on every Zoom prayer call, and living (as best as we could at the time) in Christian community.

I showed up to my first time sitting with my Spiritual Director with an agenda and a lot of cynicism and fear. The Enneagram 6 in me just couldn't help it.

The pace of life that COVID handed me caused a reevaluation of all the practices I had put in place throughout my life. Church, reading my Bible, journaling every day, all of the check-list items of my faith were now up for appraisal. Showing up to my faith throughout my life had been something that everyone expected of me. Ya know, 7th generation and all. Since 2020 I've been on a journey to sit with Jesus and ask Him what is most helpful for us, today. Coming into my faith as my own has meant that quite a few spiritual disciplines that I've used to connect with Christ throughout my life just don't serve me anymore. There have been times where I've chosen to go on a walk with Jesus rather than journal. I've taken deep, intentional, drawn-out breaths rather than pray out loud with my words. I've left my Bible closed on my coffee table, and instead had coffee with a friend, getting curious about what it looks like to sit with Jesus during this season of life. There was a renovation of the practices set in place on the second pew on the left at that church on Highway 137.

But the thing that has remained is I keep showing up to church. I love my church.

I love the story that we tell.

I love the songs that we sing.

I love the bread and the wine that we feast on at the end of every service, physically remembering that which Christ has done on our behalf.

But I also understand why a lot of people don't want to show up to church anymore.

When I was in college, 18 and freshly on my own, I did what any good church girl would do—I went church shopping. Luckily my grandma had a directory of churches in my area I could visit, so I didn't go in blind. I went to small churches, large churches, churches that held multiple services multiple days of the week. The overall takeaway from all of these churches: I agreed with and appreciated the teaching, I was familiar with the worship, but not a moment sticks out to me where someone invited me into the life of the church.

I had resigned to going to a church close to my college campus when I was in town for service times, however, being just a casual two-hour drive from home, I spent most of my weekends back at the place my ancestors planted their roots. Sunday School at 10am, morning service at 11, dinner at Grandma's house right after.

On a non-Boone Creek church day, I entered my college church, sat down in a chair, opened my journal and began to listen to the pastor teach on 2 Peter. I don't remember the full context of what was taught that night, but what I do remember is this: "Some of you are just showing up to church and taking from the buffet of what it has to offer. You aren't committed. You aren't joining small groups. You aren't contributing to the life of the church. Figure it out!!!"

As someone who showed up to this space for over a year, I realized that night it was no longer for me. The story of that church, for me, was yet again: I agreed with the teaching, I was familiar with the worship, yet no one invited me into the life of the church. I was showing up to the buffet and just looking around for someone to hand me a plate.

Could I have made more of an effort on my own? Sure. I was not proactive in that season of my life. I had grown up in a place where church was easy, and I expected it to always be that way.

Once I decided that place was no longer for me, I began the hunt for a new college church. It wasn't too long after that...well...challenging sermon that a local pastor came to speak at the college ministry I was part of. He showed up and didn't seem like an egotistical weirdo, so I googled his church and went the next Sunday.

When I first walked in a curly haired blonde lady came up to me and introduced herself. She welcomed me, gave me a bit of a rundown on what to expect, and said she was glad I was there. When the service was over, she came back. "Kayla, again, I'm so glad you were here today. I hope to see you again next Sunday!"

I've been attending ever since.

What I've found in this church is a group of people that are unafraid to admit their imperfections and are more than willing to journey together as we all do our darndest to become more like Jesus every day.

It's not a church with fog machines. It's not a church with a band of professional musicians. It's not even a church with people who show up on time. IYKYK.

But it is a church with people who show up. And I'm glad to be one of them. I'm glad to be amongst people that say hello, set up co-ed tactical laser tag nights, take new moms out to get pedicures, hug the necks of college freshman back for a weekend, and join in living all of life together. We're more about showing up to share in the apostle's teaching and break bread with one another than we are production value that can be offered to the masses.

As I mentioned, I started seeing a Spiritual Director in 2020. Showing up to church has been among the things we've examined during our time together.

Did I mention I'm a 7th generation churchgoer? I've had this physical practice of showing up to church all my life, but in recent years my spiritual rhythm seemed a little off. I was really going through the motions when it came to connecting with Jesus inside a church building. A part of me was considering if a life of faith really had to include being involved in a local expression of God's Kingdom by way of a church congregation.

As I began to examine, or deconstruct, the point of showing up to church, I began to realize that going through the motions might just be the point sometimes.

There's a story in the Bible about a woman who had been bleeding for twelve years. She had spent all that she had on doctors, unable to be healed by any. Allow me a bit of holy imagination for a moment.

One day she starts bleeding and it probably meant nothing. This happens every month.

No big deal. Here we go again.

Five days pass and it's similar to day one. Not lightening up.

Two weeks go by, she's still bleeding.

She's concerned, but not enough to go see the doctor at this point. We'll just keep an eye on it.

Two months go by, doctor's visit number 1.

"Sorry ma'am, I'm not sure what's wrong. I haven't seen a case like this before. Good luck."

Another month, doctor's visit number 2.

"Oh yes, I've come across this issue a few times in my practice. Here's some plant sap to apply. Should fix you right up."

It doesn't.

Doctors 3 through 10 offer suggestions and remedies throughout the course of 9 years and none of them work. And now she's out of money. And she's still bleeding.

So, she just keeps going about her days. She keeps showing up to her life and the way she now knows how to live it. When she gets a bit more money in the coin purse, she finds a doctor and tries one more time. None of it ever works. But the routine matters. Continuing to show up matters. Even though nothing changes, there's still a bit of hope that it will.

Then one day she hears of a miracle worker making his way through town. He's driven out demons, cleansed a man of leprosy, and even raised a woman's son from the dead! "Surely," she thinks, "if I only tough his garment this literal mess will be fixed in my body! A flow of blood should be easy-peasy for this guy!"

She goes into town, makes her way through the crowd, probably crawls on the ground and simply touches the end of his robe as he passes by.

> "Who touched me?" Jesus asked. When they all denied it, Peter said, "Master the crowds are hemming you in and pressing against you."
>
> "Someone did touch me," said Jesus. "I know that power has gone out from me."
>
> When the woman saw that she was discovered, she came trembling and fell down before him. In the presence of all the people, she declared the reason she had touched him and how she was instantly healed. "Daughter," he said to her, "your faith has saved you. Go in peace."[4]

She didn't have to show up that day. She didn't have to show up to different doctors month after month, year after year. She could have resigned to this life of perpetual bleeding. She could have reoriented her days around her ailment. She could have said, "Well, this is just what we do now."

But. Her consistency in showing up to what she wanted—physical healing—led her to show up to Jesus that day. Going through the motions day after day, month after month, year after year gave her the ability to weave through the crowd and graze the end of the Messiah's robe. Showing up full of faith led to her healing.

And again I say, going through the motions might just be the point sometimes.

There isn't a straight-line correlation between this woman's situation of blood and my church attendance. The connection, for me, comes into the practice of showing up even though you're not sure when the healing will kick in, if it kicks in at all.

At times, showing up to church became more about going through the motions than it was about connecting with Jesus. Connecting with Jesus came from morning walks, bedtimes with

4. Luke 8:45–48 CSB

miniBFFs, late nights on a friend's couch, gardening on Mother's Day weekend, bourbon in a kitchen after community group.

The act of showing up to church was to my faith what giving another doctor her last bit of money was to this woman. This is what we do now. Maybe something will shift and change. Maybe it won't.

But the point is doing it.

And somewhere along the line I realized that a life of faith really had to include being involved in a local expression of God's Kingdom by way of a church congregation.

The routine, the showing up of it all and 'just going through the motions' is what I think a life of faith is mostly about. Somehow, by the grace of God, the routine carried me through the season of disconnection. The practice of showing up kept me in a place where I was eventually able to connect with Jesus within the walls of the church again. It wasn't anything the church was or was not doing, it was simply my disconnection with what church was about.

I tell one of my dearest friends often that one of the beauties of church is we don't get to pick who we live this life of faith out with. Sure, my best friends are followers of Jesus and encourage me in my faith, but we don't all go to church together. I get to handpick my inner circle (for the most part). I don't get to handpick who sits in the maroon chairs with me on a Sunday morning.

And as we all show up together we bring so many stories of redemption along with us, and we change one another. If we don't show up, we miss that. Showing up to church does, in fact, matter.

If we become followers of Jesus that commit to consistency of life with one another, I believe deeply that the five reasons young people are leaving the church will be reversed.

Instead of irrelevance, hypocrisy, and moral failure, we'll experience vulnerability and honesty, leading to connection. This connection will lead to a recognition that God is present with His people. Safe space will be created where doubt and questions and wrestling will be encouraged, and we won't be afraid of the outcome because we know that Christ is already in it. We will learn deeply about God, ourselves, and one another. And we will knit together a community of followers of Jesus that are putting one foot in front of the other as they journey together toward wholeness in Christ, the Author and Perfector of this life of faith.

We will touch the hem of His robe together and be healed.

We won't be perfect, we won't always be on key and clap on beat, and we will probably tick some people off sometimes.

But we'll be healed.

7

To Purity Culture

The tricky thing about hindsight is that it's always better.

Also, I'm very good at judging.

According to Meyers-Brigg, it's literally part of who I am.

As a born and raised born-again Christian woman in her 30s, I've lived through some interesting times in the life of the church. Purity culture being the most prominent. When I look back over the formative years of my life, the messages I most remember are:

1—if you don't tell your friends about Jesus, they'll die in a fiery car crash (*Heaven's Gates, Hell's Flames anyone?!*) without knowing the saving power of the Gospel.

2—don't have sex.

This is about the sex.

Specifically, not having it.

Purity culture, as I experienced it, told me that if I pledged to remain a virgin until marriage, when I got married I would be blessed with a husband who was whole-heartedly devoted to Jesus and we would have mind-blowing sex from our wedding night on. It told me that waiting was worth it. That if I waited for sex, like a good Christian girl would do, God would bless that with a perfect relationship. With a man that loved Him and loved me. That I would only have to hold out during my teenage years, then all my raging hormones could be released in my early twenties once I had a ring on my finger and a marriage certificate in my scrapbook.

Purity culture promised me everything I ever wanted.

A + B = C

No sex + commitment to Jesus = virginal wedding night with hot dude who loves God and will blow your mind for the rest of your life.

Purity culture was the prosperity gospel we didn't intend it to be.

To be fair, I believe those driving the message of true love really waiting were doing the best they could with what they had. I believe that they wanted to protect the hearts of young people in the church. I believe they had an inkling of the damage that sexual brokenness brings upon humanity.

And I don't believe they knew what kind of damage their message would do to my generation. I don't believe they knew the shame and judgement, internal and external, that would reign in the lives of those of us that bought into the message they were preaching.

Again, I like to think we're all just doing the best we can with what we have. What I have now is a more fully formed view of purity and sex and the way we were designed to use our bodies and sexuality to the glory of God.

So here we go. Purity culture.

If you grew up in the late 90s/early 2000s that phrase is probably giving you goosebumps and/or hives. And for that, I am sorry.

As a product of the *True Love Waits* era, I struggle to keep my eyes facing forward every time I encounter that dreadful phrase. I already have a natural tendency to roll my eyes. Put me in front of reminders of dumbs things I grew up with, I'm likely to get my hazel iris stuck in the wrong position.

But alas, I belong to the generation of *True Love Waits*. A group of teenagers in a Nashville area church in the 1990s committed to sexual abstinence until marriage, and somehow that led to me wearing a silver(ish) band on my lefthand ring finger, vowing my virginity to my husband at the age of 14. An age where you definitely have all of your sexuality figured out. (insert sarcasm here)

I very much have a love/hate relationship with Purity Culture.

I love that it placed such a high value on sex inside of marriage.

I hate that it didn't fully expound on why it placed such a high value on sex inside of marriage.

I love that the commitment I made in a small country church during a Valentine's Day youth rally kept me from a lot of hurt and trauma as a teenager.

I hate that it took me all of my twenties and into my thirties to know and believe that my body was made for good things, and that my sexual desire was to be blessed and honored, even as a single woman.

I vividly remember being inside Lifeway Christian Stores in Springfield, MO, browsing around the turnstile displays while my mom shopped for VBS materials and coming across a small band that read "True Love Waits." I picked up the ring and read the packaging that indicated this ring was to symbolize my promise to remain pure and virginal until marriage.

FYI—according to Etsy, those rings are now vintage. L. O. L.

I wore that ring until it broke my freshman year of college and then immediately went to Lifeway and got another one.

I wore that one until it fell off my finger in the parking lot outside my dorm, never to be found again.

I haven't worn a ring on my wedding ring finger since 2010.

Praise. God.

While that ring was on my finger, what I believed most about my purity was that if I didn't wait until marriage before I had sex, God would be so disappointed in me and I would never be able to be redeemed from that sin. The vow of sexual purity was the highest form of obedience to Christ. The only motivation I had to remain chaste was so that God wouldn't be upset with me, and I could remain one of His favorites.

Being the good rule follower that I am, I dove headfirst into showing up in purity culture.

I listened to BarlowGirl on repeat and made sure guys knew that I was saving myself for marriage before they even knew my middle name. I bought all the dating books Millennials were supposed to buy, but admittedly I think I only read one of them. And it wasn't the one you're thinking of.

As I learned how to show up to purity culture—with all its flaws—I learned on some level that sex was to be taken seriously. Quite a bit of who I was in my 20s was formed by the way I showed up to purity and the culture around me.

I vividly remember a conversation with a peer during my first month of college. We were sitting in her dorm room in Irwin Hall, her and her roommate were sophomores, three of us were freshman. Her nickname was New York because she was, well, from New York.

We were all getting to know one another in the way girls do, by talking about our experiences with boys. New York turned to me and said, "So what about you?"

"Oh, I haven't had sex. I'm a virgin. And I'm not having sex until I'm married," I declared before anyone could ask.

"Ha. Good luck with that."

I dropped my head and just stared at the floor for a minute while the rest of the girls went on chatting about their escapades.

Pursuing purity started to become a badge of honor. I used my virginity as an internal judgement tool against my peers. I was better than them because I wasn't having sex.

While the movement initially occurred to emphasize sexual abstinence outside of marriage and modest dress among girls, I turned it into my predominant identity and a tool to turn off my sexuality.

Fast forward to my late 20s, I wasn't having the married mind-blowing sex I was promised when I pledged my first time to my husband at the age of 14. What I did have, however, was a sexual story that I was starting to untangle.

One of the consequences of me showing up to purity culture was that I pushed my sexual story down deep. I had sexual encounters in middle school and high school that marked my life.

I had a story with pornography that filled me with shame. I had hormones that made my body feel a certain way that I wasn't sure I was allowed to feel because I wasn't married.

Something shifted in my early 30s and I started to show up to purity culture in a new light.

In an effort to redeem all that I'd been taught, and all that I'd subscribed to, I began to get curious about my sexual story.

I was in the midst of a difficult dating relationship and some old patterns started to emerge. While I was at the park with a friend and her kids, I nonchalantly said, "I think I need to delete the web browser off of my phone. . ."

She casually mentioned a book that might be helpful called *Unwanted* by Jay Stringer.

In his book, Stringer suggests that our sexual brokenness can reveal our own unique way to healing. Part of my sexual brokenness was that I had turned my story down and my shame way up. My brokenness, or my unwanted behavior, outwardly was pornography, but inwardly it was a girl that had feelings and a body and a sexual story she didn't know what to do with.

She knew sex was good, but she wasn't sure why. Because *True Love* had told her to wait, but she waited for seemingly no reason.

A + B did not equal C. It equaled heartache and confusion and sexual desire that felt very shameful.

The truth is, I've despised my virginity at times. I went on a date with a "Christian" man once, and when he found out I was a virgin, the entire mood of the date shifted. A very real sentence that he actually said to me was, "I wonder if you'd ever be up for me just spending the night? Clothes on and everything. I just think it would be so interesting to sleep with a virgin, but like, not have sex."

I blamed my virginity, my lack of sexual experience, AND my sexually broken past as the reason I was still single. I couldn't even date someone because my sexual lack got in the way, and a new layer of shame began to form.

As I began to get curious about my sexual story, I came to realize that the pursuit of purity was about so much more than not having sex. It was about investigating the complexity that is Kayla Smith. Why does she long for the things she longs for? Why does that one line make her laugh every time? Why does she cry when people give her good birthday gifts? Why does her heart grow three Grinch sizes when she hugs her friend at a random run-in at The Fabulous Fox?

Showing up to purity culture turned into showing up to purity of life. Rather than trying to force my way into purity via lust management, I began to open myself up to purity via the movement of God into my own life.

God's heart for His people is to give a crown of beauty for the ashes we wear, a joyous blessing in the place of the mourning we carry around, and festive praise instead of despair on our faces[1]. He comes to us for our joy out of His great love. He doesn't come to us for condemnation due to our inability to measure up to a pledge we made when we were teenagers.

Christopher West writes in *Theology of the Body for Beginners*,

> God is inviting each of us, in a unique and unrepeatable way, to an unimagined intimacy with him, akin to the intimacy of spouses in one flesh.[2]

While the purity culture of my youth offered me protection from way more sexual brokenness than I did experience, I'm glad I stopped showing up to that season of my life.

Instead, I'm showing up to the process of developing a whole person pursuit of Jesus that seeks to emulate God's character, showing off His redemptive Kingdom in the world around me.

Purity isn't about chastity for the sake of getting what you want out of life.

Purity is about chasing after Jesus because He is better.

Purity that sticks around is built from the inside out, not from a sterling silver ring you place on your own finger. A life of purity forms long before the body begins to get involved.

---

1. Isa 61:3 NLT
2. West, *Theology of the Body for Beginners*, 22.

Biblical purity is better described as spiritual single-mindedness, whole-heartedness. Singularly focused on Christ.

> Come close to God, and God will come close to you. Wash your hands, you sinners; purify your hearts, for your loyalty is divided between God and the world.[3]

As we draw near with a singular focus on Christ, our hearts will be purified. It is God's presence that purifies His people. A pure heart is one that is fully alive, showing up with all its energy focused on a single end—God Himself.

> Blessed are the pure in heart, for they will see God.[4]

My 14-year-old self wanted to see God and flourish in His presence and in relationships. And the way she thought she should do that was by not having sex.

My 35-year-old self knows that to see God and flourish in His presence and in relationships is to show up, brokenness and all, and allow God to join me in the process of becoming pure, wholly focused on the light and life He offers.

Showing up to purity culture helped me remain safe in a lot of ways.

Showing up fully alive and unobstructed with Christ, broken story and all, has given me a depth of purity I only longed for all those years ago.

I want to be pure of heart because I want to see God.

Not because I want to have mind blowing sex on my wedding night.

---

3. Jas 4:8 NLT
4. Matt 5:8 CSB

8

To Family

There's a road in my hometown that my family has lived on for generations. My great-grandfather ran a general store at the bottom of the hill that led up to the homes of his sons, as well as the one he and his wife occupied. For a long time in my adolescence, I thought my family was responsible for Granny Smith apples because I had a Granny Smith. These things are logical to a five-year-old.

I also believed that Hall of Fame shortstop and Cardinal legend Ozzie Smith was kin. He, in fact, is not. I did have the chance to tell him that and he belly laughed, which validated my childhood ignorance if only for a moment.

My family has deep, anchored roots that hold a lot of life within them. The last person to sign the Declaration of Independence, Matthew Thornton, is my ancestor. Cherokee refugees broke off the Trail of Tears and settled near my hometown, making me a descendant of this Native American tribe. For hundreds of years, my family has lived out their days in the same square mileage in the Ozark Mountains. Showing up to my family means showing up to a lot.

The interesting thing about family is that you don't get to pick them. You are either born or adopted into it and you as the individual don't have much say in the process. By divine luck of the draw, I became a Smith.

Being the typical firstborn daughter, I grew up carrying the torch of doing everything the right way. I did my best in school, I played every sport that was offered to me, and I signed up for so many extracurricular activities I was able to make a double-sided t-shirt blanket out of my club involvement. I knew it was my job to make everyone proud—proud of me and proud of my family.

Like all groups made up of dynamic people, my family is a unique blend of stories that makes up a certainly wild tribe. My mom and dad were married in 1987 and not long after their nuptials, my paternal grandfather passed away. I came along in 1989 and not long after my birth, my maternal grandfather passed away. My grandmothers, whether out of necessity or proximity, I don't know, became close friends. So close, in fact, that I cannot recall a holiday where I have had to visit multiple sides of the family. It's always just been my whole family. Not only was I raised by my mom and dad, but I had the privilege of having these two strong women extraordinarily present in my life. My strength and what I have to offer the world as a woman has never been in question because I've seen womanhood modeled by the most amazing crew. I also had the honor of knowing my great-grandmother until I was 13 years old. On the day she died I was able to have a coherent and loving conversation with her, holding her hand while she told me she loved me. Lottie Mae taught me the importance of consistency in relationships (she never missed a game of pinochle or Upwards as long as she could help it), the healing power of chicken noodle soup and after school cartoons, and how to play Rack-o. I guess you could say she was the OG of showing up.

Showing up to this family as a kid was pretty easy. All I had to do was literally show up. Sure, some of the showing up was out of necessity because I couldn't drive or take care of myself on my own, but showing up isn't always just about physical presence. Being a member of my family helped form how I am emotionally, mentally, and spiritually present to my life and those around me. Sitting on the porch or at the table with the crew I grew up in offered the opportunity to learn so many life lessons. Want to know how to snap peas or shuck corn? Go to grandma's house and help her. Want to know how the Cardinals are going to fair this season? Go to grandma's and watch a game with her. Want to learn how to tell a good story, figuring out exactly when to pause for effect and land the punch line just right? Sit at any table with a Smith around it. Want to know how to be a good friend? Watch Wilma with Esther, Norma Jean, and Sonya every Friday night. Want to know how to take care of people around you? Watch Geraldine give generously of her time, talent, and treasure to those that need it.

We're all a conglomeration of the stories and lives around us, and man oh man am I lucky to be made up of all these pieces. I can see the strong through line of being who I am today because of the family I showed up in.

My dad's dad was, by all accounts from anyone that ever speaks of him, a phenomenal human being. Winsome, adventurous, and always up to something, my Grandad Kenneth was a man that drew respect from every person he met. Having been born two years into my parents' marriage, I did not have the pleasure of knowing my Grandad.

I do, however, have a picture of a young Kenneth in a sepia tone, looking off into the distance with his hat tilted just a little to the side, displaying what I can only imagine being one of the greatest characters our family has ever known.

Every time I look at this picture, with the Smith Bros truck behind him, I can't help but wonder what this man was thinking. I can't help but imagine if he daydreamed about his family—his beautiful wife at home with his children, a first-born girl and an unruly boy—and how they would all turn out. I wonder if he ever thought he would have four granddaughters—two of which knew him very well, and two that only longed for the loving embrace of a grandfather.

Growing up with the last name Smith might seem like one could get lost in a crowd, but not if you belonged to Kenneth Smith. And not if you grew up in a small town. People knew Grandad. And people knew that if you were his, your last name meant something. From what people tell me, he was a family man in highest form. Strong and steady, yet compassionate and playful. He once grounded my dad from his motorcycle because he popped too many wheelies, but when my oldest cousin decided to drive Granny's car at age 7, knocking a concrete parking bumper right out of the ground, he giggled about it.

He was a sporting man and loved to watch my dad play baseball and take him fishing. And any time I stepped off the basketball court having played a game with minimal turnovers and a handful of points in my stat line, I would inevitably hear from someone in the stands that night, "Great game, Kayla. Your grandpa would've been so proud of you!"

The kind, well-meaning phrase only added to the ache in my heart to be swept up by the handsome stranger I'd only held stories of. I longed to know Grandad the way the world around me knew him.

When I found out my sister was pregnant with her first baby, the news brought with it a wave of different emotions. Joy, envy, happiness, confusion, and longing.

The strangest emotion was that of longing, but not in the way you might think. It was longing to know and be known by my Grandad. A longing that I hadn't felt since my last high school basketball game. The longing, though, was met with great joy in knowing that this baby will get to know our dad. Winsome, adventurous, and always up to something, our dad will now be Grandad to Sister's baby. Technically, he's Pawpaw (said in the most Ozarkian accent you can think of), but toMAYto, toMAHto.

Speaking of Sister's babies.

One of the greatest privileges of showing up in my family now is as aunt. My sister and brother-in-law so kindly gifted me with a nephew and niece that have added so much delight and love into my life I can barely stand it. I had the honor of being in the room when my nephew entered the world. A gift I never knew I needed was seeing this little boy take his first breath.

He is one of the most curious and tenderhearted little boys I've ever had the pleasure of knowing. And his sister, entering this world just a little over two years after him, will rule the planet someday. She is fierce and fearless and lovely.

The role of aunt has taught me so much about what it means to steward my influence. Along with my miniBFFs, I have the privilege of living a life that is full of love and grace and mercy and fun for the sake of these little ones. I get to say yes to so many fun things that fan the flame of delight in their lives. When my nephew asks me on a Sunday morning if we can throw a party that afternoon in his bedroom, I take him to Dollar General after lunch at Granny's and we buy kazoos and balloons and army men and we throw a ding dang party. Just because it's fun to throw a party. I get to steward our joy and delight as we blow up balloons and play with new toys and find life in the moment given to us, together.

My niece recently yelled at me, with a Henri Nouwen book in hand, about how beautiful God made everything. The aggression with which she came at me was nothing short of impressive. She stared me down and exclaimed, "Kayla! God made EVERY-THING. And He made it BEAUTIFUL! You see that tree? It's beautiful! And it's beautiful because GOD MADE IT!"

Like I said, she will rule the planet someday.

As her aunt, as a person that is learning to steward her influence in the lives around her, I get to maintain eye contact, nod my head, and affirm her with, "Yes queen! You are RIGHT! God is so lovely."

Being a daughter to my mom and dad has been all the adjectives you might throw at a familial relationship. Sweet, hard, loving, frustrating, grace-filled, difficult, steady, and the list goes on. Yet showing up to who Kyle and Jen are shows me more of who I am.

My mom, Jennifer, can have a great time with anyone, anywhere. She is always down for the next adventure or the next episode of *Little House on the Prairie*. She spent her career as an educator, teaching elementary kids about health and how to have fun in P.E. class. She also coached junior high girls' basketball, volleyball, cross country, and track and field over the course of her tenure. To this day, athletes that she helped develop hug her when they see her in Walmart, ask her how she's doing, and write tributes on my dad's Facebook page when Coach has a birthday[1]. She retired from teaching full time and the first thing on her list was to plan an August trip to Chicago where she and I spent two nights in the Windy City, walked 10 miles in one day, and had a hotdog at Wrigley Field. While waiting in line for a beverage she casually mentioned something about the time she went to Tijuana with her college basketball team. I gave myself whiplash as I spun around to ask more details, having lived 33 whole years of my life now realizing my mom was a rebellious collegiate. She proceeded to reassure me that they were playing in a tournament in southern California and crossed the border just to go to the beach. I'll believe her. For now.

She went on to become a member of her alma mater's Hall of Fame with that basketball team. I had the privilege of going to the induction ceremony where I got to meet so many of her teammates, hear story upon story of their camaraderie on and off the court, and watch my mom deliver a speech about how special of a time in her life that season was. Pun intended.

I also got to tag along with mom when I was an only child to a volunteer position she had with Independent Living for foster children through the Missouri Department of Family Services.[2] At least once a month, I would travel with my mom to a central location in our county where 5–8 teenagers would gather together for a couple of hours and learn some basic life skills from Jennifer. She spent some of her evenings teaching these humans how to budget, run their laundry, and make a spaghetti dinner. Food nights were my favorite. I didn't realize until a few years ago how special it was that my mom gave of her time to love these kids *and* that she brought me along too. Most people might shy away from their 5-year-old sharing space with 'troubled' teens, but she wasn't. She

---

1. My mom refuses to have Facebook, mostly because she was a teacher and she has wisdom, but she also does have my dad's password and uses it frequently to be in the know with the goings on in the world.

2. Now known as the Older Youth Program with Missouri Department of Social Services.

brought me into their lives, and them into mine. I'm sure I picked up some life skills beyond how to make some pasta myself.

Bottom line, Jen is down for anything. She brings the fun, the conversation, and the energy to every day. I've learned how to have fun in life and give away love because of my mom.

My dad, Kyle, is strong, principled, and consistent. He gets up at the same time every day, no matter what lies before him. He feeds his animals, gets himself ready, and goes to town for a cup of coffee with all the other men that gather before starting their workday. Kyle is the sneaky one of the family. He might be the funniest (tied for first with his mom), but you have to be paying attention. He's also known for sticking his ice-cold hands on your neck when he comes in from feeding the cows on any given winter's morning.

If ever there were a guy that showed up to the people he loves by serving them, it's my dad. He will tinker and fix and mull about with whatever free time he has. He'll show up to a friend's house to work on their tractor at the drop of a hat. He'll make sure neighbors' animals are fed so they can go on vacation. He is a steadfast man, and I'm grateful to have grown up in his household.

He's also never known a stranger. Throughout my time as an amateur softball player there would be at least one instance every weekend where we couldn't find my dad. He would inevitably be standing near the tournament bracket posting, figuring out all the scenarios we could wind up in should we win or lose. We would walk up and see him hamming it up with some random person, also deciphering their daughter's pool play outcome.

"Who was that?"

"Oh, that was Don. From Columbia."

"How do you know Don?"

"I don't. I just met him. His daughter plays for. . ."

Proceeds to give us all the information he has about his new best friend, Don.

I've learned how to speak respectfully to my elders, look someone in the eyes, and shake their hand with a firm, confident grip from my dad. He taught me the value of hard work and how good the end of the day feels when you've given your all to the task at hand. I've learned how to hunt, fish, and pay attention to the world around me. I also stand with my right foot crossed over my left, with my hands in my pockets, just like my dad.

Sister is who I want to be like when I grow up. If she's afraid, she doesn't show it. With seven years between us, it took a lot for me to grow out of older sister protector/wannabe parent into simply sister. Watching her grow up, I saw someone that knew what she wanted and always went after it. She does not take no for an answer—for better or worse. One Christmas evening, she had been begging my parents to let her go to her friend's house for a sleepover. My mom repeatedly told her no, because it was Christmas night and she wanted us to all be together. There would be other nights for sleepovers.

About thirty minutes later headlights shone through our big living room picture window.

Out walks my sister with a bag packed.

She had called her friend and told her it was fine for her to sleepover, but her mom had to come pick my sister up.

She's never taken no for an answer.

She's also business minded and always thinking up ways to creatively fill needs around her, willing to take risks in ways that give me second-hand anxiety. In early May 2022, she called me and asked what I thought about her starting a mobile coffee shop.

"I've looked online and there's a trailer I can buy. I think I'm gonna do it."

"I mean yeah, that would be really cool, but do you have a business plan? What's your timeline? Where are you going to put it?"

I continued to ramble on with my million+1 questions.

"I don't know, I'll figure it out."

Three weeks later I received a Snapchat of her truck pulling a coffee trailer behind it.

She opened Grady Rae's Coffee Co. on rodeo weekend in my hometown and hasn't looked back. It's one of her three businesses.

She is brave and strong-willed and so so smart. When she was little and you asked her what she wanted to be when she grew up, she always answered with, "I want to play volleyball, work in a mall, and cut hair." And she has done just that. Her athletic ability only amplified her drive to be the best at what she does. In college, she worked at Bath & Body Works in the local mall, and honestly, I'm a little frustrated that I never got a discount on a three-wick candle. And now, her primary business is as cosmetologist. She washes, dyes, and cuts hair while she listens to people's stories, offering a word of advice if it's asked, or simply a space for people to decompress and talk things out that they've been holding on to since their last visit in her chair. She is kind and compassionate, but also. . .won't take no for an answer.

Have I mentioned I want to be like her when I grow up?

This is just scratching the surface of those of us who make up the Smiths. I could tell story after story about the people beyond our immediate family, on both sides. Maybe that will be book #2. As I'm writing, I'm realizing what a gift it is to show up to my family. Not everyone gets the opportunity to live life connected to those that share genes. And sometimes, jeans. Yet, we don't have to show up to our family to be formed. We are already made up of the stories that come before us.

For those of us given a family that we can show up to, there is tremendous opportunity to grow even deeper roots in the lives we've been given to live if we choose to show up in the system we were birthed into. As a daughter I've learned how to trust those in authority over me, a privilege I recognize deeply because the parents I have are good parents. As a sister I've learned how to love, fight, cheer, respect, challenge, and be challenged. As a granddaughter I've learned how to be generous, how to tell a story, and how to make a graham cracker pie. As a niece I've learned that adults other than your parents have great capacity to love you. As a cousin I've learned how to laugh. As an aunt I've learned how to deal with part of my heart walking around in the outside world, trusting that God cares more about their life than I could ever dream of. As a sister-in-law I've learned how to trust another person with someone you love more than you can explain and take great delight as you watch him care for, love, and build up your dearest loved one.

The way I show up to my family has changed tremendously over the years. For the longest time my dream in life was to go to college, become a physical therapist, and move back to my hometown to practice my craft. I was the daughter that would move back home and plant roots in the plot of land she grew up on. I went off to college and my plans quickly changed. No longer on the path to become a physical therapist, I found myself in a city and community that I really enjoyed and after college I decided to stick around. My role in my family was still the same—first born daughter, older sister, granddaughter, etc.—but the way I showed up to that role started to shift. No longer was I just physically present everywhere my family was. I had to figure out what it meant to show up to my family while I was also leaving the nest and creating a family of my own.

There aren't a lot of playbooks in life that we can refer to as we grow up and grow out of old patterns and ways of doing things. If ever I wanted a playbook for how to do life, it was during the transitional period from college to full-on adulthood.

After graduating college, I moved in with some friends from church and got a job. I started to spend my weekends and free time in the city I lived and worked in, adjusting to life as an adult on her own. Being a tight-knit family, there were expectations that I would spend my non-working weekends on the farm, helping with chores, sharing meals, going to church, and then returning to my new home on Sunday evening. I, on the other hand, was trying to spread my little baby bird wings as I left the nest, hoping I would figure out how to fly.

The fun thing about me in that season of life is that I wouldn't communicate. Rather than telling my parents up-front that I was staying in St. Louis for the weekend, I would just avoid them. I would dodge their calls and texts and then let them know late on a Friday that I wasn't making the trek this time around. I didn't know how to tell the people that I loved most in the world that I didn't want to be around them. But it wasn't because I didn't want to be around them. It was really because I was trying to build my own life, make my own friends, find my own footing in the world.

One Saturday night when I didn't ignore them, we went out to dinner just the three of us. Olig's BBQ was the restaurant of choice. The food that Maria and her family served is still second to none in my mind.

On our way to the restaurant I brought up the elephant in the room: I needed to feel the freedom to not be around as much, and I needed them to know that I didn't love them any less, I just needed to become my own person.

Both of my parents responded with such love and kindness, understanding that I was, in fact, a grown woman. Or at least trying to be.

But they also didn't let me off the hook for my crappy behavior toward them. They still parented me and my 23-year-old self, reminding me the importance of letting people in on your life, communicating what you need when you need it, and remembering that this is a family worth showing up to.

It was one of the hardest conversations I've ever had with my mom and dad, yet transformative in our relationship. They knew that I knew I wasn't 16 anymore and it was time for us all to start treating me that way. But also, I will still call my mom to ask where I can find the honey in the grocery store. We still need our parents to be our parents.

When I think about being a Smith, I think about the image of Jesus weeping for the city of Jerusalem, longing to gather them together "as a hen protects her chicks beneath her wings."[3] Having grown up with hens that gather and protect, this metaphor is highly relatable. I have been able to live my life gathered up under the wings of Jesus because I was lucky enough to be born a Smith. With all the stories and lives that have come before me, I am made up of broken people that have stumbled their way through life, doing their best with all that they have to leave a legacy worth leaving behind.

3. Matt 23:37b NLT

My family isn't perfect, but I'm so glad this is the one I get to show up to.

9

To Pain & Grief

"Hope is never foolish; it is always brave."—Margaret Fay

Starting an essay about showing up to pain and grief is weird. So, here is my messy way of jumping into an uncomfortable part of my story.

I turned 35 this summer. I am currently not married, and I currently do not have any biological children. I do not own a home. I don't have a sexy career. I am my 13-year-old self's worst nightmare.

13-year-old Kayla's ears rang with the refrain of the well-known Psalm 37:4 (ESV)—"Delight yourself in the Lord, and he will give you the desires of your heart."

She set out on a quest to delight herself in the Lord, no matter the cost. Because delighting yourself in the Lord meant you got what you wanted in life. And what I wanted/want is a husband, children, mortgage, and to not have to be the only one to decide what we're having for dinner tonight. Or the only one to take out the trash. Or the only one to grab toilet paper on the way home.

Every endeavor to delight in Jesus held the undercurrent of longing for the desires of my heart.

Fast forward 22 years—I do not have the desires of my heart.

What I do have is a lot of pain and grief that I am left to hold.

I have felt behind in life since I was around 26. My friends were married, were having kids, and were buying houses. My 19-year-old sister had just started dating the man she would end up marrying 2 years later.

The whole "delighting myself in the Lord" was working out for everyone but me. Self-pity became my modus operandi.

Leading your life with self-pity is, turns out, a pitiful way to live. I went on for a while grasping for any semblance of 'moving forward' in life, only to be let down again and again.

Eventually, I got over my self-pity, thanks to friends that pointed out the good things I had going for me. I watched my sister get married and my dad do the Wobble with his cell phone in its belt clip on his jeans. I watched my friends have babies and brought them buffalo chicken sandwiches in the hospital. I helped friends move and pack up their kitchen, teaching them how to put their hanging clothes in trash bags so they would travel easier. I turned my life outward, showing up for those in my orbit and finding great delight in doing so.

I was doing this for everyone else, but I wasn't doing this for me.

There was still the undercurrent of being behind.

My dad wasn't doing the Wobble at my wedding.

I wasn't having babies.

I wasn't moving into a new house.

I was just. . .showing up.

One of the gifts of living in St. Louis is Forest Park. On June 24, 1876, 1,371 acres of St. Louis countryside was officially dubbed Forest Park, crushing the size of Central Park in NYC by 500 acres. One thing St. Louisans love to boast about is the 1904 World's Fair[1].

The only Fair structure that remains today is the Saint Louis Art Museum. Boasting works by Monet, Van Gogh, Seurat, and

---

1. You're welcome for the popularization of peanut butter, ice cream cones, and cotton candy.

others, the Art Museum welcomes in visitors to beautiful galleries, impressive collections, and free admission.

Yes—you read that right—free admission. Nearly all of Forest Park venues offer free admission. The one place that isn't free—that is coming to mind right now—is the Boathouse, which is a restaurant. And if college economics taught me one thing, it's that there is no such thing as a free lunch. That's why St. Louis is one of the best hidden gems in America.

My favorite painting that has been on display in the Art Museum is *Christ and the Sinner* by Max Beckmann (1917, pictured below).

This painting depicts the story of the woman caught in adultery in John 8. Religious leaders bring a woman before Jesus that was found with a man that was not her husband. Where the man was, we don't know. This story isn't about him. Trying to trip him up, the Pharisees say to Jesus, "Yo—this lady had been adulterating. What're you gonna do with her?"

Jesus, in the way He does, bent down and started writing in the sand, and when they weren't satisfied with his silence, they got a lil rowdy. His response? "If you've never sinned, pick up a stone and throw it."

In my mind, reading/hearing this story growing up, I always pictured it to be a docile scene. More of a mild meeting of the minds in the corner of the town square than a face-off in front of a crowd.

I can't tell you the first time I saw this depiction by Beckmann, but when I did tears came to my eyes. There was animosity in the air. People were frustrated. I was so captivated by the protection offered by Jesus, by the clinging of the woman, by the tension of the crowd.

And when I saw that painting, I saw myself kneeling behind Jesus, clothes torn, defeated countenance.

I started to feel my grief for having delighted myself in the Lord but not having the desires of my heart.

This image woke something up in me that needed to be tended to, but I just wasn't ready. I just kept starting at the piece of art with tear filled eyes.

Something about longing for the desires of your heart is that you're nearly always looking for ways to fulfill your own desires.

This recently came about by way of crushing on a guy in my orbit and then being crushed by him. For better or worse, he is Mr. Flirtatious. After months of passive flirting, me putting myself in his way, and him laughing at all of my jokes, I finally sat him down at a coffee shop and said, "Hey. We connect. I think you're amazing. I like you and I'd be really interested in seeing where this goes."

After a long conversation and a few weeks for him to process, we sat down again and he told me, essentially, "Thanks, but no thanks."

My delighting in the Lord had once again left me without my desires. I started to see a pattern.

I got my hopes up.

I expressed my hopes.

I got crushed by my hopes.

I felt like a fool.

At one point or another, the hope becomes too much. It is too hard to bear another let down. Another day of delighting in the Lord only to go to bed with no one beside you.

A couple of years passed, I got over my orbital crush, I had been in and out of relationships, and I was fighting tooth and nail to continue delighting in the Lord.

My life felt stagnant. And then, in the fall of 2023, it started to feel like my life was going from stagnation to a downward turn. My car engine blew up, literally. I got so sick I coughed my rib out of place, literally. I couldn't drive anywhere. I couldn't workout the way I was used to. I just couldn't bear it anymore. I got so sad and so frustrated.

And all my sadness and frustration was with God.

His presence and nearness was never a question.

The question was, "What are you going to do about this?! I am behind your leg, begging you to not just protect me but pick up a rock and throw it at THEM!"

Not long after I took a dip, I found out that Mr. Flirtatious was engaged. It literally came out of nowhere considering I didn't even know he was dating someone.

Not that I was entitled to that information, but due to our proximity and the number of conversations we'd had over the course of time, I would've thought something like that would come up.

And shockingly (to me) it wrecked me. I wasn't holding on to any assumption or aspiration that we would end up together, but something about him moving forward in life opened the pathway for all the grief I'd been holding to come flooding out.

The friend that broke the news felt horrible.

The friend I texted reminded me to be kind to myself. To choose the good narratives as I feel the painful emotions.

I spent the entire day at my desk weeping.

I could attach the picture I took of myself at 4:01pm on that day, but you'll have to buy me a drink to see that one.

The grief poured out.

The darkness showed up.

> When it (darkness) comes, it does not have the character of something, but of nothing. It is like long afternoons in childhood when it is raining and there is nothing special to do. Darkness shows us the unresolvability of things, opens up the possibility of being permanently at loose ends. It seems to be going on forever. Yet our faith is still present and we know God is there. He is there, but the bush does not burn. We know God is present, but we have no sense of him. Darkness is unsensation. It is neither bitter nor sweet. If we were not believers, we would despair.[2]

The unresolvability, the unsensation hit me like a ton of bricks. I spent the next 36–40ish hours completely numb.

It wasn't him being engaged, but it was.

It wasn't my friends being married and having babies, but it was.

It wasn't my sister's business success, but it was.

It wasn't all these things for all these other people, but it was.

I was delighting myself in the Lord. *Everyone else* was getting the desires of their heart, or rather, the desires of *my* heart.

I cried out—literally—to God and just asked him to freaking show up (PG version). I asked Him to give me what I want. Those of us who are evil, when our children ask for bread, we don't give them a stone. . .so aren't You supposed to give us so much more?!

2. Griffin, *Clinging*, 22–23.

This news his me on a Thursday, I spent time with my dearest on a Friday, and I worked out on a Saturday. My modus operandi of self-pity in more recent years has included beating my body to a pulp by way of multiple classes at my gym. On the Friday, my friend offered the opportunity to break out of normal patterns—rather than punishing myself for something out of my control, I could offer myself kindness. I could actually show up to my pain and my grief.

So I did. I chose a better way for myself, and that way included going to the Art Museum to see *Christ and the Sinner*.

I went to a Hot Pilates class, showered, grabbed my book, journal, and water bottle, and headed out to the Art Museum, straight for the Max Beckmann.

I walked in the front doors, turned left into the first main gallery, and. . .no Max Beckmann. No *Christ and the Sinner*.

I stood there, stunned.

I said out loud in this quiet museum, "You've got to be kidding me."

It was literal crap icing on a mud cake. I showed up specifically to see this painting and it was gone. Not on display. Replaced by something else I can't even recall.

I was pissed.

I sat down in the chairs in the middle of the gallery and started journaling about how annoyed I was, how mad I was that I just never get what I want. Internally yelling at God about how much of a jerk He had been—did He not see all that I was giving to Him and He couldn't even give me a freaking painting?! Could He not, just for this one time, give me what I wanted??

After getting out some rage and taking some regulating breaths, I pulled out the book I brought along with me and started to read.

Clinging: The Experience of Prayer by Emilie Griffin was the book of the day. Gifted to me by a sweet friend, I began to read words that would communicate my frustration and longing and heartbreak in ways I really needed it to.

After an hour or so, I finally got up to browse the rest of the museum. I think there's something to be said about slowly walking through an art filled space, intentionally taking in hundreds of years of creativity. Walking among beauty is healing.

I made my way into one of the European galleries. Slowly moving amongst the gigantic paintings, I suddenly was stopped in my tracks.

There she was.

Christ and the Woman Taken in Adultery.

Painted by Mattia Preti in the 1640s, she hung there in oil on canvas, an astounding 56 5/8 x 75 ½ in. She brought immediate and overwhelming tears to my eyes.

All of the grief and frustration I had been feeling for the last few days—well, few years if we're being honest—was met with the kindness of God hanging on the Art Museum wall.

He gave me what I asked for, just not how I asked for it.

He gave me Jesus. And he gave me the woman caught in adultery.

He didn't give it to me the way I thought He would or the way I wanted Him to, but He gave it to me. He gave me what I needed.

I work really hard at delighting myself in the Lord. I don't say that arrogantly. It is *work* to delight in the Lord, but it is worthy work that I want to spend my lifetime doing. As He and I work together to grow that delight, He shows me in His ever so loving kindness that He does, indeed, give me the desires of my heart. In the same way He gave me Christ and the woman caught in adultery, He gives me intimacy, companionship, purpose, unconditional love, mothering, and so much more, just not how I pictured it or asked for it.

Being in the Art Museum that day was such a lovely reminder in the midst of my pain to continue to hold on to hope. That showing up to pain and grief is also a practice of showing up to hope.

And showing up to hope is a tricky thing for me.

Hope hurts.

Hope asks us to hang on when everything around us tells us that hanging on makes no sense.

That's why hope is brave. It asks us to show up when showing up might let us down.

In showing up to my pain and grief, I had to put hope away for a little bit.

When I'm doing a reverse lunge while holding a kettlebell (my actual hell), there are times when I have to set the kettlebell down. It becomes too much. My back starts to hurt. My form gets thrown off. I just need to set it down and do the reps without it.

So, I do.

And when I'm ready to pick it up again, guess where it is?

Right where I sat it down.

That's hope for me. Amidst pain and grief, I set it down.

Get insurance with God and do a good deed, settle down and stick to your last. Keep company with God, get in on the best. Open up before God, keep nothing back; *he'll do whatever needs to be done: He'll validate your life in the clear light of day and stamp you with approval at high noon.*[3]

In the midst of heartache and grief, I sent my friend a text, "I feel so foolish."

She responded, "I don't know if you can hear this right now—but hope is never foolish. It's always brave. You are the most brave."

Hope is never foolish. It is always brave.

Showing up to pain and grief and the very real risk that hope might let us down yet again is the bravest thing I've ever done. I think it's the bravest thing any of us can ever do.

And while I do have a lot of pain and grief left to hold, I'm holding it *with Jesus.* Just like the woman, I'm clinging to his leg, bent over in desperation with tattered clothes and a tear-stained face, and the Man of Sorrows Himself is right there with me.

3. Ps 37:3–6 MSG, emphasis mine.

10

To The Gard

"Can I call you my farmer friend?"

"Huh?"

"Like, if someone asks, 'Where'd you learn that?' I can say, 'my farmer friend Kayla told me.'"

"Oh. Yes. I am your farmer friend."

I lived and worked on a farm for 18 years. Well, maybe the better way to say that is I grew up on a farm and had chores to do. I know some things about some things when it comes to farming. And, by proxy, gardening.

March 16, 2020, was the last 'normal' day I would spend in my office. I spent the last 2 hours of my workday grabbing books and computer accessories to take home for a makeshift workspace that I would probably use for just a couple of weeks until we all went on with our lives.

COVID-19 had another idea.

Two weeks went by, and my makeshift workspace turned into the place I would spend the rest of the year working from.

It's currently December 14, 2020, and I go to my office to check the mail. That's it. COVID has done a lot of damage for a lot of people, and that's the nice way for me to put it. It has ruined lives, disintegrated relationships, and torn communities apart. This isn't about COVID, but it gets a weird shout-out because it brought me to The Gard.

The Gard, as it was affectionately called by a brown-eyed two-and-a-half-year-old miniBFF, began in the spring of 2020 in a small patch of dirt next to my friend's patio. We mulched, planted flowers, and landscaped in the front of her house—a project that we absolutely crushed in one day—then we moved on to the veggies.

Spinach. Snack sized peppers. Peas. Tomatoes.

On Silent Saturday we worked the ground and planted the seed.

And so began a project that I thought I was just coming along for the ride with, but that garden began to do something in me that year.

You see, the thing about gardening—or planting anything, really—is that it is a process. It can be tender, it can be slow, it can be harsh, it can be fruitless. What you put in the ground determines your process. For our little patch of land, the process would be simple. Water. Weed. Wait a few weeks.

One of my favorite moments was a bit of a surprise to both of us. We chose to put some snap pea seeds in the ground—a veggie that we both like to eat but had never grown. Those suckers took off and took over their little dedicated section of dirt. At the beginning of their budding, my friend and I snapped one off, popped the pod open, and ate the fruit of our labor together. We both got that wide-eyed emoji look on our faces, followed by a, "Wow that's good!"

The process was paying off.

Tending to The Gard was a living parable I was being invited into. As previously mentioned, COVID sucked for a lot of people. But it illuminated the story I was walking through in ways that I didn't expect. The forced slowness of the world kept me from Cardinal baseball games, shows at the Muny, Friday night movies on Art Hill, backyard BBQs every other night of the week. I was forced into slow rhythms with few people.

When you plant a seed, you don't get to time lapse forward and eat the fully formed snap pea in a couple of hours. You put the seed in the ground, cover it with dirt, water the dirt, feed it the proper nutrients, and wait.

You keep waiting.

Keep watering.

Keep watching.

Keep tending.

And then wait some more.

If you're lucky and you've done it correctly, at some point you'll walk out to your garden and see little sprigs of green popping out of the dirt. You'll wonder, "Was that there yesterday?" The tiny, tender shoot that came from seemingly out of nowhere will give you renewed hope that a harvest is coming. So, you keep waiting.

We see so much imagery in scripture about gardening/planting/harvesting. Not only were our first parents placed in a garden with their Creator, Christ wept in a garden before redeeming humanity, and ultimately we will all live in a garden filled with the presence of God. This deeply agrarian text that followers of Jesus spend their time unearthing the story of God within teaches us a lot about God's process of nurturing.

> The Lord planted a garden in Eden, in the east, and there he placed the man he had formed. The Lord God caused to grow out of the ground every tree pleasing in appearance and good for food, including the tree of life in the middle of the garden, as well as the tree of the knowledge of good and evil.[1]
>
> The Lord God took the man and placed him in the garden of Eden to work it and watch over it."[2]

One of God's connections with His image bearers was for them to take care of the creation He had established and upheld. This is a connection we can still embrace today. When we look to the physical world around us—the dirt, grass, flowers, crops, wildlife, streams, clouds, people, etc.—we see not only the handiwork of God, but the outworking of what He has been cultivating all along.

1. Gen 2:8–9 CSB
2. Gen 2:15 CSB

With The Gard, my friend and I were offering quiet care that we believed would lead to fruitfulness, a prayer of hope that what was buried in the ground would produce great beauty.

This is what God offers to humans—His abundant love given in quiet care, producing good fruit in the lives of those that daily walk through death of self in hopes that beauty will grow in the soil that He is tending.

I spent all of 2020 focused on hope. It was my word of the year, and my longing was to find it renewed in Jesus. To expectantly wait for Holy Spirit to heal me and resurrect some living hope in my life.

I buried the seed of that hope deep in my soul and covered it with dirt. Not because I was trying to smother it out or ignore it, but because I needed to care for it.

I watered it with quality time, holy conversations, movie nights with friends, and reading books to miniBFFs at bedtime. I watered it with weekly laundry sessions at my friend's house while we drank coffee, bore each other's burdens, and took tiny boyfriends to the "jungle" in their park.

And I waited as days rolled right into one another, the only thing changing being which coffee mug I would drink out of that morning.

And I watched as, slowly, tiny sprigs of hope started to sprout.

That's the thing about the holy work that God does in the lives of His people—He plants, and covers, and waters, and waits. He quietly tends to His Kingdom.

But the difference between He and I is that He knows when and what will sprout up.

The long, slow, steady, and faithful process is one I have come to love because of The Gard. In the same way that farmer friend Kayla and her partner in veggie-crime watered the small patch of dirt next to a patio in the city, God was watering the dirt in my body when my hope was buried with so many small moments of abundance throughout 2020. The abundance didn't come from grand adventures or life-altering events. It came from steadily showing up with God and the people that love me. The Gard has helped me to slow down and find relief in the pace, rather than anxiety and frustration that everything isn't happening all at once.

It's early 2021 and I'm sitting at the dining room table of the house where The Gard was planted. Two miniBFFs/tiny boyfriends are asleep upstairs while their parents are at the hospital welcoming their baby sister into the world. I'm staring out the window where The Gard lies currently dormant in the winter just on the other side, teary eyes, savoring this moment.

This is abundance. This is the garden of hope growing.

My spiritual director once asked me, "What if the tears of abundance are watering the garden of hope?"

The answer? They are.

The hope isn't ready to snap off and take a bite out of quite yet, but it's getting there.

And as I sit in the abundance tonight, I can't help but wonder what springs up out of the ground in the morning.

Farmer Friend Kayla and her faithful friend are still digging in the dirt, planting veggies, and waiting to see what will happen. We're currently in the middle of season five in the tiny plot of land that lay next to a concrete patio on Cornell.

This will officially be our last season on Cornell as this crew is moving to a new home. Don't worry, they're going from 7 minutes away to 15. The Gard will live on in some form for seasons to come.

And don't tell my parents, but I have come to love this practice. What I used to loathe as a kid—getting out in the middle of a hot day, pulling weeds, harvesting veggies, dragging the hose out to hook up to the sprinkler—I now long for. Well. I long for a version of that. The upside to our city setup is that there's not a lot of weeding to do, we handle things when the outside isn't so hot, and the hose doesn't have to be drug that far.

What I'm really longing for, though, is the rhythm. The Gard has planted in me just as I have planted in it. As I've mentioned, this cultivating of the dirt has mirrored the cultivating of hope in my heart.

The operative word here is cultivating. There is work to be done. And yet, the tension lies in the hope. With hope, you don't necessarily work. It's more of a passive awareness of what you're longing for.

The tension of working while also waiting is necessary for both The Gard and hope.

Whether you plant a spinach seed or a seed of hope, you don't see it sprout immediately. We've talked about that.

But my current problem is that the spinach in The Gard year 5 is not doing so well. And the hope in my heart is not doing so well.

The spinach is sparse. Some leaves have poked through, but they look terrible. They are small and weak and probably won't make it.

And if I'm honest, I'm afraid of that being the story of my hope. While The Gard is in the middle of the summer season, my hope is in the dormant cold of winter.

Hope and I have a tricky relationship.

With gardening I mostly know what to expect.

I rarely know what to do with hope.

According to my internet dictionary, hope is: "a feeling of expectation and desire for a certain thing to happen."

It's no secret that I have had strong feelings of expectation and desire for a certain thing (or things) to happen. More than 2 conversations with me and you will likely hear some version of, "Yeah, I want to get married and have kids."

And for a long time, I fully expected that to happen.

Now, I'm not so sure.

As time goes on and I creep deeper into the second quarter of my life, I'm not so sure I expect the thing(s) I want to happen will happen anymore. And yet, I still desire them.

So, what do you do with hoping yourself out there. With opening yourself up to your desires when the story you've lived in tells you that you'll probably be let down?

How can the tears of abundance continue to water the garden of hope?

With actual plants (not the metaphorical one I've been running with), you can overwater them. You can saturate them to the point that they get root rot, discolored leaves, mold, gnats, and stunted growth. The water takes up too much space in the soil and there's no more room for oxygen, which in turn damages the roots to the point they are unable to take up water.[3]

There are days, weeks, months where the leaves of my hope have been discolored. My soil needs a bit more oxygen in order to properly nurture the seed of hope that has taken root.

With gardening there are often multiple routes to take when caring for a plant. If overwatering isn't the issue, it might be the time of day you're watering it. Or the nutrients in the soil. Or the plants around it. Or unexpected extreme temperatures one way or the other. And the work of the gardener is to figure out what the problem is and address it.

And so, as the apprentice gardener, I take my plot of soil in my heart and my plant of hope to the Master Gardener. I invite Him to show up to my Gard and help me figure out how to tend to this precious little seedling inside.

And He does. He assures me that the tears of abundance are still the best way to water this plant. He pulls some weeds out, He rearranges my watering schedule, and He offers some new nutrients to work into the soil.

The Gard is a living parable.

We plant.

We water.

We tend.

We wait.

And so does He.

As the seasons change, and the purpose of the ground changes along with them, what remains is that the gardener is always at work. We're thinking about what kind of fertilizer to add to the ground during the fall/winter to make it more fertile for next planting season. We're plotting ways to keep the deer out of plants. While the ground is dormant the work is not.

3. Insert a new line into that Alanis Morissette song.

And so it is with God.

While hope may lay dormant, the work to strengthen it, sustain it, grow it, and see it come to full fruition is still happening. The Gardener is still at work, doing exactly what needs to be done.

In the same way I show up to The Gard with my friend, caring for and cultivating this sweet little hobby of ours, I show up to The Gardener who cares for and cultivates the ground in my life, watching and waiting for something beautiful to sprout up.

11

To The Light House

Since I graduated college in 2011, I have lived in 5 different places. A townhouse with 3 other ladies, a house with 2 roommates and a grapevine in the backyard, an apartment behind an IHOP, a house with 1 roommate, and The Light House.

No shade to everyone else, but The Light House is my favorite. I've been living there for five and half years and the life we have lived together is quite wild.

I moved into my apartment to live on my own for the second time when I was 29 going on 30. I packed boxes with way too many coffee mugs and on the most beautiful, sixty-degree January Saturday, my friends, boyfriend at the time, and I loaded up a U-Haul van and headed 5 miles northwest to my new dwelling place. It took three trips in that van to get everything from one place to the other, and once we were done, all of my belongings were piled in the middle of my new living room floor.

While the men and I were in between residences, my besties were at my new place unloading kitchen items and gawking at how many mugs I own. To this day none of them buy me coffee mugs as a gift because they know I am not lacking in that area. 7 people gave up their Saturday morning to help me move my life into my very own one-bedroom apartment with plaster walls, archways, and a movie theatre within walking distance.

My seven-years-old at the time miniBFF joyously exclaimed, "Wow! Ms. Kayla! Your department is beautiful!"

She wasn't wrong.

Initially dubbed 2S, I sat out my *Deathly Hallows* welcome mat (a gift from my bff) and got to living my life in my new city dwelling. At the time I had a boyfriend of four months and a lifetime ahead we were anticipating together. I arranged my bedroom, bookshelves, tv stand, and rocking chair just right, realizing that I had absolutely no eye for design. I'm a function over form kinda gal.

My first night in my new apartment I slipped in the shower and bruised my backside. A shower mat was the first purchase I made for my new home.

One of the things this new dwelling brought me was a deck. A 6x10 space just off my kitchen overlooking my neighbors back yards, the deck quickly became a space where I loved to spend my time. Facing the east, I would plop my bag chair out in the morning sunlight, sip on my coffee, and slowly wake up to the day. Journaling, reading, sitting, the deck turned into a sacred place.

Growing up in the country, one of the things I didn't realize I missed was simply sitting outside. Lingering on the back porch after a long day with my parents, rocking in a porch chair. Sharing meals with neighbors in the summertime on benches and in the grass, occasionally taking a break for a dip in the pool. Being outside was more important to me than I realized.

The deck at The Light House opened me back up to what showing up outside can do for me. Getting that morning sunlight on my face or closing out the day with a movie and a glass of wine, being outside on the deck slows my pace and allows me to be just a little more present than I was the moment before.

The bag chair turned into a COVID summer project of a pallet chair featuring cushions that the squirrels eventually ate the insides out of. We then transitioned to bonafide deck furniture, thanks to my summer birthday and my parent's willingness to buy a 32-year-old an early present.

I now have a second-floor oasis of my own, seasonal plants, permanent tv stand, and squirrel protection included. Turns out, the space you dwell in matters.

Back inside.

The Light House wasn't always The Light House.

For three years it kept its initial name of 2S. Since my move in date, I've rearranged my living room three times. I've added a bar cabinet, coffee table, rug, and IKEA shelving system. This past summer my mom and I hung my tv on the wall. I've never felt more grown.

My bedroom has been moved around and I got a new mattress. And thanks to one of my stimulus checks, I was able to add a freestanding bathroom cabinet.

2S transformed into The Light House little by little.

During the second iteration of the living room floor plan, I was in a terrible relationship. He was not kind. He did not respect me. He. . .well. . .was an abusive boyfriend.

One of the rhythms of our tumultuous relationship was that he would come over to my place twice a week—on Tuesdays and Sundays. We spent 75% of our time together in my living space.

The naming of The Light House came from this relationship. Or rather, this breakup.

The day after the worst night ever, my best friend came over with coffee to listen to me word vomit and offer up her presence in the midst of my breakdown. She compassionately sat with me and listened, while lovingly inserting her wisdom and care when necessary. As our time together ended, she prayed for me.

"Lord, as we sit here, I can't help but notice all of this light. . ."

And there it was.

The Light House.

I learned how to live in the Light of Christ in The Light House.

The Light protected me in ways I didn't know I needed protection.

As layouts and rugs and bathrooms changed, so did I.

The prophet Isaiah wrote about the coming salvation for Zion. The Lord is promising to enter in and shift the atmosphere for His people.

> No longer will they call you Deserted, or name your land Desolate. But you will be called Hephzibah, and your land Beulah; for the Lord will take delight in you, and your land will be married.[1]

The space that we dwell in matters. The space that the Lord takes up in our dwelling matters. In the renaming of His people and their land, God reclaimed beauty and honor for His people.

By naming my second story square-footage, my friend reclaimed beauty and honor for me.

A few months after the breakup, another bestie came over for an impromptu walk around the neighborhood on a day off. I had been sending her Amazon links for a few days of couches I wanted to buy because I was just sick of mine. I was ready to ditch the college IKEA feel and move onto a grown-up Ashley Furniture vibe. When she arrived, she quite literally walked in and said, "Oh. No. We're not doing this."

Remember when I said I was function over form? She's form over function. We need each other.

The neighborhood walk got delayed as we spent the next few hours rearranging my living room for the third time. We shifted the couch under the window, the bookshelf under the sconces, and the tv on top of the bar cabinet on the interior wall. She told me to buy a rug, so I did.

She not only shifted the space I lived in, but she helped to continue the shifting in my heart as well. You see, I didn't really want to spend thousands of dollars on a new couch to spruce up my apartment. What I really wanted was a space that didn't remind me of a terrible season of life. I wanted a new name.

Being function over form, I tend to get stuck in what is. I don't always think creatively about ways to get out of my own way. I had been living in this space that this man and I had shared a lot

1. Isa 62:4 NIV

94

of terrible time in, where a lot of damage had been done, and when that was over I left it exactly how it was. It worked. Everything fit. The space didn't need an adjustment. There was nothing wrong with the space itself. The old name suited it just fine.

But the space reminded me of everything that happened in it.

When my friend came over and quite literally flipped it all around, she set me up for healing I didn't know I needed.

Now, when I sit on my couch under the window, my view is of my wall where the light pours in and illuminates the department with loveliness.

The Light pours in and illuminates my heart with loveliness.

The naming of The Light House occurred a few months before the rearranging of The Light House, but isn't that how it is with Christ too?

God never asks us to offer Him a perfectly curated dwelling place to inhabit. Rather, He declares that He is moving in and doesn't mind the state of the flooring.

In the book of Revelation, one of the encouragements given to those that remain faithful is that they will receive a white stone with a new name written on it that no one knows except the one who receives it.

The promise of a new name comes before we get to the destination. There's significance in speaking words of life over the space we bring ourselves into. It's not lost of me that one friend declared my home a place of Light and another set me up to actually receive the Light within it.

No longer Desolate, rather Delight.

No longer 2S, rather The Light House.

As light has a tendency to do, The Light House has exposed, warmed, revealed, and provided nourishment that I didn't know I needed. The double-edged sword of living on your own is that there's no one else around. It's lovely because I can leave the dishes in the sink for as long as I want to. It's potentially destructive because I can leave the dishes in the sink for as long as I want to.

Living in The Light House these past five and a half years, I've really had to learn what it means to live with myself. There's no one else around to help me be the person I want to be on a day-in-day-out basis. This space has exposed my apathy, most significantly on display when the junk mail is piled inches deep next to the coffee station. It warms my spirit when the big Christmas light bulbs are perfectly positioned inside my living room window. It reveals my loneliness on a Wednesday night when I come home to midweek chores that only I can do. It provides nourishment when my friends come over for a movie night and we're snuggled up on a tiny couch that three grown women have no business being on.

Maybe more than anything, I have learned how to be on my own with Jesus in The Light House. I have built a dwelling place to be with my Faithful Friend. I have learned what everyday life can look like when I take time to notice that He is nearer than my next breath. He is with me when I brush my teeth, when I leave for the gym, when I make my coffee, when I pack my lunch, when I lounge on my couch, when I just don't feel like vacuuming again, and when I lay my head down to rest, preparing to do it all again tomorrow.

The Light House really is exactly what it says it is. A place full of light and Light. Showing up to the Light every day is a gift I hope I never take for granted.

12

To The Little Ones

My favorite internet friend, Annie F. Downs, introduced me to my favorite descriptor a few years ago: miniBFFs. A term coined for the offspring of grown-up BFFs, it's one that I have adopted into my everyday vernacular. As a never-married non-parent, I have the privilege of really sweet relationships with my friends' kids. Ranging from 19 to 1, I've lived a lot of life with those that Jesus says the Kingdom belongs to.

My first foray into having miniBFFs came with two little boys whose parents hosted my church small group. It wasn't too long after we started our weekly meetings that mom and dad announced they were pregnant with baby number 3 and this one would be a girl! She's now on her way to being taller than me within the next 6–10 months.

A lesson that I learned with this OG group of miniBFFs is that talking to kids as if you're talking to an adult is the most fun thing to do. I would show up early on a Thursday night before the rest of the group arrived, sit down at the kitchen table, and ask six-year-old Maverick and three-year-old Goose about their days. Goose was known for a scowl and a cold shoulder, which only made me love him more, but Maverick would pull up a chair and chat about the library book he picked up that day. He would tell me about his friends, he would tell me about the games he loved playing, and he would share his life with me. The only obligation I had was to pay attention, to show up and just be with him.

As time went on Goose started to like me, and Penny turned into the personification of joy. In 2018 I went to Orlando on a work trip and made my way to some of the resorts. Penny was, at the time, rightly obsessed with Ariel, so naturally, I bought her a key chain to hang from her backpack. When she got on the bus the next day, she proudly proclaimed, "My grown-up friend Miss Kayla gave this to me. She's the best!"

Life with this crew was more than just a Thursday night and a Sunday morning. It was familial. I became Auntie Kayla, and the Lord started to show me that my grown-up presence in the lives of these little ones matters.

I just got home from a Laundry Day Friday, which is exactly how it sounds. On Fridays I go to my friend's house to do laundry. It's a tradition born out of COVID-19 and me not wanting to wash my clothes in a laundromat during a global pandemic.

This LDF started out just like any other: I show up, throw my clothes in the washer, and we hang for a bit before her 2 eldest children wake up. However, after the toddlers got up from their nap, this one in particular took a turn.

Baby sister (a fresh 5 weeks old) did not want to be put down for a nap. Middle brother was frustrated with elder, and I could not console him.

Mom came downstairs and gave me the job of sitting with baby sister while she fell asleep. Rock her, hold her close, help her calm down.

What I thought would be a 15–20 minute snuggle sesh turned in to nearly 2 hours of being under a baby because she just did not want to be put down.

And about an hour in, all I could do was pray. Pray for her. Pray for me. Ask God for His wisdom in stewarding my influence and my life for the sake of these little ones. Not because I need to be made great in their eyes. Rather, because I know that I have the opportunity to make His love known in their eyes. Baby sister nestled up in my neck, breathing her baby breaths, sighing her baby sighs, feels safe with me. Middle brother bumps his forehead up against mine as we stare into each other eyes and make weird noises, and he feels safe with me. Elder asks me to sit down with him for dinner, and he feels safe with me.

According to The Fuller Institute, intergenerational relationships are one key to building lasting faith relationships among kids as they transition from adolescence to adulthood[1]. Kids greatly benefit from having five or more safe adults in their life that not only love them and support them but reinforce the worldview that their parents are modeling in their home. It only makes sense, for me, to invest in the lives of my friends' kids (my miniBFFs) and to steward my influence in their lives in a way that honors my friendship with their parents and brings glory to God in the process. Showing up to the little ones gives them a wider place to land when they fall. Sure, their parents are (hopefully) the primary source of safety and reassurance, but if you've had a parent, you know how much they annoy you and get in the way. If I can be on the outer edge of the family circle, offering love, care, rebuke, and support, then praise God.

And that's why showing up to these little ones matters. They feel safe with an adult that is not their parent. When they are older—as one of the OG miniBFFs is—they will, with God's help, feel safe enough to tell me what they want to be when they grow up.

Feel safe enough to tell me about the crush they have at school, or which teacher annoys them the most.

Feel safe enough to tell me when their mom and dad are just being so dramatic and unreasonable.

Feel safe enough to listen to me when I tell them how precious and valuable they are in the sight of their Creator.

And feel safe enough to hear me when I tell them that I love them with my whole being, and they truly believe it.

Those of us that are non-married, non-parents aren't off the hook when it comes to the little ones. Our words matter. Our

---

1. Powell, Griffin, and Crawford, "The Church Sticking Together," 19.

presence matters. Our ability to rock a baby to sleep while her mom has uninterrupted time with her brothers matters.

It's not just an obligation to friends to show up for their little ones.

It's an honor to show up with the little ones. To the little ones. For the sake of the little ones.

One Friday I was hanging with miniBFFs while mom did some work things. It was November, so colds and sniffles abound. We watched some Babu and very sweetly entered nap time. The oldest two are champs, so they hopped into bed while I made a bottle for the littlest and she and I snuggled until deep sleep hit.

Everyone's asleep for about 10 minutes, then the oldest starts coughing. I gave it a couple minutes, and the cough continued. I was nose deep in a book that I really wanted to crush during uninterrupted quiet time, but this sweet little one just could not catch a break with his cough. He was sad and asking for mom, so I did the next best thing—I grabbed his water and snuggled with him in bed.

He took some sips, sullied up into my shoulder, and shed a few more tears. We took some deep breaths together. He sipped some more water. His cough became more intermittent, and we both fell asleep on the bottom bunk with his brother snoring sweetly above us. I could've slept there for 4 whole days if it weren't for the wooden bed frame pressing into my skull.

What a gift to nurture this sweet human. What a gift to provide comfort for this little boy. Tears can't help but roll out of my eyes when I think of how sweet of a gift we are to each other.

But showing up to the little ones is about way more than what I can offer them.

Kids will offer us more life than we can imagine if we let them.

I have tattoos. One of my favorite things is when my mini-BFFs notice them. There are some candles that little boys always try to blow out. One member of the crew spent a solid two years pointing to the inside of my biceps every time I saw her, exclaiming with her pacifier in her mouth, "Tattttoooooooo!"

One afternoon I was playing with my little buddy who was 3 at the time and he caught the word "Beloved" peeking out of my t-shirt. As I slid my sleeve up for him to observe the ink in its entirety, before I could say anything, he asked, "Does that say Kaka[2]?"

Going against every instinct to correct him, I simply answered, "Yes, that does say my name."

In a simple interaction on a random afternoon, this little boy reminded me that my name is Beloved.

These little ones offer us more than we can ever imagine.

There's a scene in the Gospel of Matthew where Jesus is in the middle of some of His teachings and parents show up with their kids, hoping that this man called Jesus could lay His hands on them and pray. The disciples scolded the parents for bothering their Teacher.

> But Jesus said, 'Let the children come to me. Don't stop them! For the Kingdom of Heaven belongs to those who are like these children.' And he placed his hands on their heads and blessed them before he left.[3]

Showing up to the little ones teaches me what it means to show up to the Kingdom of God.

Growing up, I used to think that when Jesus was talking about the Kingdom of Heaven belonging to those that are like children, what he meant was more along the lines of those that called God their Father could have access to the Kingdom. Like, yeah, we're His children, so His Kingdom is ours. As I've had the privilege to be around kids more and more, I realize the depth of what Jesus was talking about is almost unreachable.

Kids are some of the most curious creatures I know. They ask "Why?" until they are satisfied, which is almost never. They smell things and put them in their mouth to figure out what the heck is going on. They investigate, they explore, and push buttons they don't even know they're pushing.

2. Kaka is my nickname because this boy couldn't say Kayla when he was 18 months old. My prayer is that I will be in their contact list as Kaka when they're all adults.

3. Matt 19:14–15 NLT

You never have to wonder who a kid feels safe around. When they're learning to walk, they go to the safest person in the room—often their mom or dad. They bonk their head? Straight to mom/dad's lap. A stranger enters the room? They hide behind their grown up's leg, allowing just one eye to peek around the corner at this new person they're sharing space with.

I re-learn one of my favorite lessons I've learned from showing up to the little ones every time bigBFF makes one of them mad. Watching my friend parent one day, she firmly yet lovingly told her oldest son no. He tried to bargain with her to get what he wanted, and she held to her denial of his request. Offering multiple bids for compromise, he ended up not getting what he wanted, and he burst into tears. Immediately, he went to his mom, who also happened to be the source of his hurt. She held him and hugged him close as he buried his head into her shoulder and told her how unfair her decision was. He allowed the person that hurt him so deeply to be the one that comforted him.

After a couple of minutes, and a distraction provided by little brother, he left the kitchen and I said to my friend, "Man, isn't that exactly what God desires of us when we're pissed at him?"

When Jesus said that the Kingdom belongs to those that are like children, I think this is exactly what he's talking about.

Jesus invites our curiosity. He wants us to ask "Why?" until we're satisfied, which will hopefully be never. He wants us to investigate, to explore, to push buttons. Kids are able to do this in the context of safety, which is exactly what Christ offers. Our curiosity can be held by Jesus because he is the one that upholds all of creation. God is not caught off guard by our questions, our doubts, or our prodding. In the same way that we delight in the little ones coming to us as they figure out the world, I believe the Father delights even more when we come to him as we try to figure out the world.

In the same way that kids run to their safe people, Jesus invites us to run to him. As we're learning how to walk in the new shoes that lead us down the path of following Jesus, his arms are wide open, ready to catch us as we stumble and inevitably fall along the way. In the same way I looked at my miniBFF while she was learning how to walk, Jesus looks at me with delight and love in his eyes, hoping to see me succeed in the task at hand. He's not disappointed in my stumbling. He picks me back up and helps me try again when I'm ready.

And the hardest lesson to implement in my own life is my favorite one I've learned. I'm not sure I would have the relationship with God that I have if it weren't for watching my friend make her kids mad. Seeing the little one run into his mother's arms for comfort after she was the one that hurt him woke something up in me. I took my observation from my friend's kitchen into my prayer life and have put into practice the act of burying my head into the shoulders of God, letting him know how hurt I am and how much I'm expecting him to fix it. Watching this little one not only be comforted but be able to go on with his day after such an egregious hurt, gave me hope that I can do the same. The only requirement on my end is to come to Jesus like these little ones.

We spend our lives trying to grow out of childhood. The invitation from Christ is to grow into it. To learn how to come to him the same way they come to their safe people. To learn how to be curious, not afraid of the questions or settle for an answer that's just a little unsatisfactory. To learn how to let the one who loves us with a love that we cannot even comprehend be our ultimate source of comfort, care, and ease.

For me, these lessons are not learned outside of showing up to the little ones. As grown-ups I think we can get way too focused on only showing up to our grown-up friends. Kids can seem like an unfortunate logistical puzzle to work around as you figure out how to function in adulthood. The truer reality is that we all need each other. We all learn from each other. And when we all show up with and for each other, we get a greater picture of what it means to be part of the Kingdom of God, of which belongs to those who are like these children.

13

To Waxing

I got a Brazilian Wax for the first time in my life as a 32-year-old, never married, extraordinarily private, self-conscience woman. I'll spare you the details, but the main motivation behind it was a skin issue and I was testing a theory about the presence of hair. Because that's what you do when have perfectly capable doctors to talk to about these kinds of things.

That's a weird way to say that I really didn't have a reason other than itchy skin and curiosity.

I have a friend that I have declared a lot of "nevers" to. A lot of things that come up in discussion that I adamantly put my foot down and determine to never take part in—waxing was one of them. The ironic thing is that, to date, I have now done every. single. one. of. those. things.

A few months ago, after another "never" had turned into a "this is what I do now," she jokingly mentioned that if I ever got waxed it would be the ultimate accomplishment in her using her powers against me. For good or evil, we still haven't determined.

One of those nevers was going on a run. I don't love running. And I really don't love running with other people, mostly because they are better at it and I'm very insecure. She and I went on a Sunday run before the Midwest humidity got the better of us. After I got home, had a moment and a cup of coffee, I sent this text:

"Running with someone is so so far out of my comfort zone. Thanks for saying yes today. It meant a lot."

"As always—it's a pleasure to be a part of things you swore you would never do. May there be many more!!"

You see, it's not the running that is hard. Well, yes, it is. But it's showing up in a vulnerable state. Putting yourself in a position to be seen in ways you aren't confident in. Exposing your weaknesses. Showing another human the space where you lack, when, despite your best efforts, you don't want to be someone that lacks.

And in that exposure, there is tons of risk. Will I look foolish? Will my friend think I'm incapable of doing this 'easy' thing? What if I really can't do it? What if all my fears come true? What if this is the thing that finally proves I'm not as valuable or capable as I thought I was?

Yes—that's a lot of pressure to put on a Sunday morning run that I asked my best friend to go on with me. But that's the tactic of the enemy, right? Take something that you've done at least a hundred times in the course of your life and tell you all the lies you've ever given attention to will become truth in an instant. And the real kick in the metaphorical nuts of it all is that you're doing it with someone that has already seen you at your literal worst. Who has held you as you weep. Who has called you on your bullshit. Who has entrusted you with their life. THAT PERSON—the enemy tries to sow a seed of doubt with.

But what the enemy doesn't know is that with every "never" we kill those lies. With every act of vulnerability that waters the roots of soul-connection, he loses. Whether it's a Sunday run with a friend who is a few strides ahead but never out of sight, or a wax with a stranger that you can't help but laugh about for a week—every act of vulnerability proves that life lived with people is a way more flourishing life than one lived in isolation.

So, yeah, I got a Brazilian Wax, and I sent a Marco Polo to my friend where I did nothing but giggle and quote *Lose Yourself* by Eminem. It was so painful, yet I didn't die. It was so vulnerable, yet I wasn't rejected. I mean—I was a collegiate athlete and hadn't been as exposed as I was on that wax table! The main motivation may have been to life-hack a skin issue, but I knew I could do it because I had lived through all of my other nevers.

I knew that I had a safe place to land if it went terribly.

And I knew that I had the ultimate "never" to utterly shock my friend with if it went . . . well . . . as good as it could go.

There's a scene in the Gospel of John where Jesus is serving His disciples, washing their feet and giving them some parting words before His arrest in Jerusalem. He tells them that He is the vine that they are to remain tethered to. They are the branches. As long as they are attached to the vine, they're safe. They will produce what they are meant to produce. They will be cared for by the Master Gardener. They will be pruned and tended and will do exactly what they were made to do in this world.

They can show up because they are tethered to the safety of the Vine.

I showed up to waxing. I showed up to a Sunday morning run. But ultimately showing up in these spaces of safety solidified my tethering to the Vine. I am able to live my life more fully because of others being present and showing me who I am, all of us branches abiding in the Vine where we can all be seen, cared for, and continually show up for each other. And we can all face our nevers because our attachment to the Vine is secure in Christ.

You are greeted with so many surprises when you allow yourself the freedom to fail and be uncomfortable. All you have to do is show up. And what a gift it is to knock nevers off the list in the company of those that want nothing more than to see you flourish into who you were designed to be.

14

To Singleness

"The cave you fear holds the treasure you seek."—Joseph Campbell

I never thought I would be 35 and writing about still being single. The grief and pain of it all has been covered, and the longer I live in this state of unmarriedness the bigger those two feelings get, yet showing up to my singleness is about so much more than what I don't have.

I started writing and putting my words out onto the internet almost 11 years ago with the express purpose of talking about singleness. I had gone to the *Storyline Conference* hosted by Donald Miller at Belmont University in the fall of 2013 with my friends Benji and Jess. I was dabbling in the writing game but hadn't quite found my voice or my story. I knew I loved writing but wasn't totally sure what the point of my writing was.

During those three days on a lovely college campus, those of us in attendance were faced with the question, "What will the world miss if you don't tell your story?"

On the drive home, Benji, in his Marine Corps veteran gusto, said to me, "You're a writer Kayla. You have a story. Write it."

And so I did. I spent the rest of that drive and the next few weeks figuring out what I had to offer to the world. As a 24-year-old female steeped in the world of Christendom, what I had to offer was my take on singleness. The initial subtitle of my blog was, "an irregular discussion on relationship status."

The discussions I had about singleness in the church always revolved around how hard being single is, or how the season of singleness was simply meant to turn me into the wife I would one day be. Even then, I was tired of those conversations. The story I believed the world would miss if I didn't tell it is that there is so much more about who we are other than our relationship status, and that if we're going to have a conversation about our relationship status, there's a more lovely way to have a discussion that doesn't end with someone telling me that I "just need to fall in love with Jesus before I can truly fall in love with a man." *Insert face melting emoji here*

Week-in-and-week-out I wrote blog after blog about what single life was like. Looking back, I truly believed that I would blog about singleness and somewhere along the line, probably by year 2, I would meet someone and the discussion would take a more domestic turn. I couldn't have imagined that 11 years later I would still be showing up to my singleness.

Yet here we are.

And, as Benji said, I'm a writer, so I'm going to write about it.

Being a single person in the evangelical Christian world has been one of the weirdest roles in life I've ever held. Growing up I was very clear on the idea that marriage was the end-all-be-all for us Christian gals. The ultimate expression of our femininity was as wife and mother. The church I grew up in made this point stick deep in my psyche with every Mother's Day church service they held. Each year, potted hanging plants would adorn the altar at the start of service. Songs would be sung, announcements would be made, and then the pastor would stand at the pulpit declaring how important motherhood is. He would then ask all mothers to stand and would call out categories, asking those that didn't fit to sit down. Those plants were given out to: Youngest Mom, Oldest Mom, Mom with the Most Kids, and Mom with the Newest Baby.

The story that was communicated to me: if you're a wife, then you're a mom, and then you matter.

So, my heart held on to the day that I would walk down the aisle of that church and pledge my life to my husband, and with any luck the following Mother's Day I would be walking out with a hanging plant.

It never crossed my mind as a teen that singleness would be the status I would bear this far into my life. That wasn't how life worked. You lived through high school, went to college, met a boy, and got married. You didn't get past the age of 25 without a ring on your finger.

So, showing up to my singleness has been tricky to say the least. Yes, there's been loss, but there has also been great gain. No one could've prepared me for the abundance God would have to offer me *because* of my singleness.

When I was a freshman in college I went to tennis practice with a mentor that coached a local high school team. These high school girls were, expectedly, interested in a college girl's love life. When they asked if I had a boyfriend, I proudly proclaimed, "No, I'm actually taking this time to date Jesus."

Oh, sweet baby girl.

She was cringy, but her heart was in a tender place.

Singleness in my late teens/early twenties offered me the opportunity to do just that—get to know Jesus. Because I wasn't spending all of my time with whoever I was dating, I had the time to learn what my life with Christ could look like. I developed a practice of journaling. I studied my Bible. I read Christian authors. I learned new worship songs on my guitar. I dove headfirst into making my faith my own, as Kayla. Not as Kayla + a boyfriend that she thought she was going to marry. My lack of dating allowed me to be formed with Jesus and no one else, which is a gift I treasure to this day.

I once heard a Bible study leader say that people would only be truly sanctified once they got married. That the relationship between husband and wife was the ultimate opportunity to be faced with your own sin and selfishness, to offer your own love in sacrifice, and to be loved fully by another who saw all of your flaws.

In my best Dwight Schrute, "False."

Singleness offers the same thing. The difference is, when you're single, you have to be willing to show up. I've never been married, so I can't really speak to what that life is like, but I can say that in singleness, it really easy to hide. It's easy to pick and choose who you show what to. Singleness requires a level of vulnerability because there's no one else around to show you your blind spots. You have to be willing to open up your life, (metaphorically) naked and (literally) unafraid, allowing yourself to be seen by God and safe people who love you. At its best, that's built into marriage. I can confidently say that I, as a single woman, have been faced with my sin and selfishness. I'm faced with it every time I want to hang out with my friends and they can't because their kid has a specific nap time, and my annoyance rises to the surface. I get to offer my love in sacrifice every time I'm asked to do anything and I say yes when I'd rather say no and just go get some chips and queso by myself. And I'm able to be fully loved by another who sees all my flaws because I've done the work to show up in all my mess with the people I'm fortunate enough to live life alongside. That's not a humble brag, it's just the honest to God truth. I don't know how to live any other way. I want to be more fully human in the presence of Jesus, and the only way I know how to do that is to come before other humans around me, honest, open, full of gaps in understanding of the world and myself, and willing to risk the connection AND fracture in relationship.

Singleness has taught me how to do this. If I were married, I'm not so sure I would know how to be the Kayla I am today. And I really like her. She loves deeply, is a steady presence, and (hopefully) displays the kindness of God on her good days and her bad.

Okay, back to first person point of view.

Singleness has also been a crash course in boundaries and stewardship. I definitely did not sign up for this course and I would like to speak to my academic advisor about how I got enrolled as soon as possible.

There's a misconception that single people have all the free time in the world. We don't. Sure, we don't have a spouse to consult or kids with schedules to direct our time, but we're not just sitting around waiting for you to ask us to do something. When you're single, you have more options on how to spend your time. The question is, are we spending it well.

In my 20s, as a lonely, figuring it out, single lady, I jumped at any opportunity to spend time with people and/or tasks. New at my job, I did whatever I could to prove myself, which often included earlier mornings than required, and later nights that were unnecessary. Not only was I trying to prove myself, but I was also making sure that the way I was spending my time mattered. If I wasn't at home with a husband or kids, then using that time to work was the 'right' move to make to express my value to the world. Having any kind of free time wasted on me just sitting down to take a breath meant that I was lazy and not doing what I could to further God's kingdom.

Luckily, that didn't last long.

Crash course in boundaries and all.

I quickly realized that running at that pace served no one. Learning how to build in space for me to settle into the life that Jesus and I had built in college was tough. I'm not sure if you've ever built fence, but if you have, you know that the process is grueling. You usually wake up pretty early to beat the heat, gather your equipment and head out to the fields. If you're lucky, you have a tractor with an auger on the back. If not, handheld post hole diggers it is! You slam the tool into the ground, clamp it together, and pull up the dirt. On a good day when the ground is soft, this will take a few minutes per post hole. Then, you set the post, make sure it's level, fill the hole back in with dirt and if you're fancy, pour some concrete to make sure it's set. A few days later, you come back to your perfectly lined fence row and start stretching some wire, barbed if you grew up like me[1].

---

[1]. I lived in perpetual fear that the barbed wire would snap back and rip my backside wide open. I think my dad told me only one time that I needed to be careful, and I carried that tiny warning with me certain that I would

After a demanding process, the fence is built and the boundary lines have fallen in a pleasant place. The cows stay put. The horses stay safe. Everything is as it should be.

Building fence around your life isn't much different. Especially when you're the only one around to do it. The gift that marriage offers is that you move into a new property with the fence already built. You're not necessarily blaming your boundary lines on your spouse, but from an outsider's perspective it's way more understandable that you can't jump at every opportunity because there's more than just you involved in the decision-making process. When you're single and stretching the wire on your own, you might get some sideways looks.

But building the fence is important to keep the property in order. The fence helps us recognize which cows are ours and which aren't. What is mine to say yes to and what isn't.

And that's where stewardship comes into play.

As I learned how to walk back all of my insecure yeses, I began to know more fully how I am made to contribute to this thing called life. One of my greatest prayers of the last few years is that I would steward my time and my influence well. As a non-married non-parent, I have a unique opportunity to steward my life in ways a lot of those in my world don't. I can pick kids up from school. I can come over to watch the older two because the younger one just randomly broke his leg and you have to take him to the ER. I can spend my money on a random trip to Hawaii to see a friend and snorkel in the ocean while the whales sing their songs. I can tip the waiter 100% (on a $16 bill, don't get too impressed with me). I can wake up early to go mow my friend's lawn before they get back from vacation. I can take people to the airport. I can show up to church to serve. I can go to NYC on a whim because a friend's work trip allows for free lodging.

I can literally do whatever I want, as long as it's in line with the life that Jesus and I have built. And that is one of my favorite parts about showing up to my singleness.

---

be maimed every time I helped him with this task. Being an Enneagram 6 is exhausting.

And also, there are so many times when I want my singleness to go away. I want to stop showing up to my unmarried self.

Singleness is hard. On one hand, I get to do whatever I want with the time that I have. On the other, on days when I need to come home and just get a hug, I can't. And I'm not here to say that so we can all get some party favor and throw a shindig on behalf of my pity. I'm saying that because it's true. God Himself even says so.

> After God gives man this directive, He realizes something is missing. It is not good for the man to be alone, so I will create a companion for him, a perfectly suited partner.[2]

One of the reasons I think singleness is so difficult for people like me is that we, as evangelicals, do not have a good theology around singleness OR community. Most of the sermons I heard growing up that had anything to do with being single were focused on how you can grow into a good spouse. There was more emphasis put on the domestic life of a husband and wife within the walls of their own home, while a robust view of communal hospitality was lacking.

For those of us that follow the Way of Jesus, marrieds and non-marrieds alike, we have to be willing to step into a connected life with one another. Showing up to singleness has been more bearable as time goes on because the people in my circle are willing to show up to their lives as well. It's not just about how do we live life within a marital status, but rather, how do we live life together as the people of God, because again, He has said that it is not good for us to be alone. I'm convinced to my core that the greatest tactic the enemy uses is isolation. If he can get us alone, whether it be alone in an apartment on a Friday morning, or alone in our bed next to our spouse on a Tuesday night, he will do his darnedest to whisper attractive lies telling us that no one sees, no one cares, and no one will come. Showing up battles against the hyper-individualized culture that we as Americans seem to exist in. The most effective way to tell satan to suck it is by living a life

2. Gen 2:17b-18 The Voice

wide open with God and the people around you. It's not for the faint of heart. It's not just for single people.

It's for those of us that long to be more fully human in the presence of God and His creation.

The overall conversation around relationship status hasn't changed much in the last 11 years. What has changed is the way I show up to it. I'm still a little bit jaded and cynical and eye-rolly about it all, but I'm also more curious when people offer me the opportunity to grow into the wife God would have me to be. Rather than write that person off as someone who just doesn't get it and never will, I can practice what I preach and invite them into showing up to their assumptions about it all. I can offer my story and put the abundance of Christ on display, even though to some I might be living in lack. I can ask them about their hopes and dreams in life, rather than being satisfied with a surface level exchange about what school their kids go to.

Showing up to singleness has shown me that there is way more to life than what we do on the outside. Intimacy, self-awareness, love, sacrifice, joy, longing, nearness, and grace are available to all of us as we sit with Jesus and learn who we are in Him, and in the presence of His people. Again, as Jospeh Campbell said, "The cave you fear holds the treasure you seek."

If the cave of singleness holds the treasure of abundance for me, I'll show up at its mouth every single day. Pun intended.

15

To Myself

It's a Tuesday afternoon and I'm sitting in The Light House, staring at a Woodwick candle flame, streams of light pouring onto my living room gallery wall, with a YouTube video providing some lakeside ambience, complete with a fire pit and pumpkins scattered on the virtual ground. I'm trying to find the words to write when I think about showing up to myself.

A lot of the work in showing up is discovery. You find out who people are, what places are like, what ideas exist, how you can navigate your presence in the world and with those you live life with. When it comes to me, the discovery part of showing up is an interesting one to consider.

I was born to Kyle and Jennifer in the summer heat of 1989. I don't exactly remember what all took place that day, but I'm sure it was spectacular for all involved.

One of my earliest memories is when I was around four years old. We had gone on vacation to North Carolina to spend some time on the Outer Banks. I was walking barefoot and stepped in some glass, which turns out, is not fun for a four-year-old. I remember, vividly, sitting in the car while my mom consoled me and cleaned out the boo-boo on my foot, then I proceeded to walk as if my foot had fallen off for a few steps before I realized everything would be okay.

Another early memory I love to pull out of the bank occurred with my cousin Lisa when I was around the same age and she was working at a Lee's Chicken.[1] I was hanging out with her for the day, and she needed to go pick up her paycheck, as this was way before the time of direct deposit and ADP online portals. We walked in and one of her coworkers said, "Lisa! I didn't know you had a kid!"

"Oh, she's my cousin," a startled Lisa replied.

"Ugh, mom!" retorted a hilarious comic-to-be, Kayla.

I've always been cautious, and I've always been funny, if I do say so myself.

On another trip to North Carolina my mom and I went for a walk to the basketball courts near the beach house. As I dribbled down the road, she told me I was going to be a big sister. "I hope it's a boy," I so kindly responded. Spoiler alert, it was not a boy.

A few months later, on the day after the coldest Fourth of July I've ever personally experienced, my sister was born. My grandma took me to the hospital to meet her and I got to eat my mom's cafeteria meatloaf. I was equally thrilled about both.

With seven years between the two of us, I began to live life as older sister to Emily. I was no longer the kid that got to walk down the road, dribbling a basketball with her mom as she went. I was now my sister's keeper. I was paving the way. It was my responsibility to show her the ropes, to keep her safe, and to occasionally change her diaper because mom was at night school and dad had a weak stomach. I remember my mindset shifting when I became an older sister, taking on the role of vigilant daughter.

I've always been a curious skeptic and "old for my age" as most of the white-haired ladies I grew up around would say. Whether it was tinkering in the garage with my dad or trying to figure out how to ride a skateboard on a gravel road, I wondered how the world worked. I was on the lookout for things that would harm me and those I love. I was fiercely loyal to my friends, and always ready to throw my boots on when my dad would ask me to go help him with something in the field. I was present and I wanted to belong. I knew what was expected of me and I tried my

1. Lee's Chicken has the most superior fast-food biscuits. Fight me.

best to live up to those expectations, even if they were only placed on me by me.

Thinking back on my formative years, I was living so many different lives, trying to figure out which one I wanted to stick with and actually live out. I think most of us find ourselves in that position as teenagers. Our brains aren't fully formed, we have different social groups at school we're navigating, adults telling us what to believe and (hopefully) why to believe it, and often we're just trying to make sure we smell good so the boy we have a crush on notices us. Being a kid is hard work.

For me, in junior high especially, I had a string of negatively transformative moments that settled into my identity. I had words spoken about me that settled into my psyche, and I worked so so hard to become the opposite of what they said. My multiple lives became even more engrained into who I was: athlete when I needed to be, good legalistic Christian girl when I needed to be, studious teacher's pet when I needed to be, girl trying to prove herself when I needed to be. I was constantly trying to live up to the day at hand, when looking back, all I wanted to do was just show up to it.

This kicked off a season that lasted well into my twenties where I did my darnedest to make up for my sins. It was really hard for me to believe that God would accept Jesus' sacrifice as an atonement for my sins. I was always trying to pay my own debt, even though the tab had already been covered. I lived life hidden and secret and as one might imagine, it was not good.

I went to college and my hidden life started to thrive. Turns out, when you live in a dorm room without adult supervision, and you have no community around you, and you aren't doing anything to combat the darkness you're facing, it's easy to hide.

I was playing softball, but I had lost all joy in the sport. I had a roommate, but she was with her boyfriend most nights. I went to a campus ministry, but it turned out to basically be a cult. I sank deeply into myself and was complacent living life the way I was living it. I would skip practice because I told my coach I had homework. I would dodge my parents phone calls because I was supposed to be at practice. I would skip class because I just couldn't muster up the energy to go. The lies piled up and the ability to keep the whole thing running was slipping away. It truly is only by God's grace that I have a bachelor's degree.

In February 2008, I went to a weekend college retreat with an organization I had just recently started an internship with. I would spend Friday to Sunday with other collegiate athletes, growing in our faith and connection with each other. Like most overnight Christian retreats, we had a quiet time built into the schedule. I went to my little corner in the basement room I was sleeping in, laid on top of my sleeping bag, and opened my Bible to the book of Hosea, a book I had only discovered that day as I ran my fingers down the Table of Contents.[2]

I came to the seventh verse of the second chapter, and I started weeping.

> She shall pursue her lovers but not overtake them, and she shall seek them but shall not find them. Then she shall say, 'I will go and return to my first husband, for it was better for me then than now.'[3]

When the text said "she" it was really saying Kayla.

In that moment I met the girl I wanted to start showing up to.

I met the girl that knew she had to return to her first husband.

I met the curious, skeptical, funny girl that had been chasing so many different secret lovers but was ready to return home.

So, I did.

I drove the two hours home to my parents' house and told them I thought I need to quit softball. That I was so sad and miserable and this thing that I once loved so much was, I believed at the time, the source of my problems. My dad, in one of his best moments, looked me in the eyes and said, "If that's what you need

---

2. If I'm being honest, the only reason I chose to read it was because I had never heard of it and I assumed no one else had either. So, when they asked me what I read, I could say, "Oh, just the minor prophet Hosea," and I would blow everyone away with how holy I was.

3. Hos 2:7 ESV

to do to feel better and to be happy, then do it. We support you. We're proud of you no matter what."

My dad gifted me the ability to begin to show up in my life again.

God began the process of helping me shed the layers of all the secrets I was keeping hidden. He began to show me what grace really looks like. He has faithfully given me Himself and His people to help bring out the best in me without having to perform or show up as who I think they want me to be. He has remained faithful to a bride that still hides, but the hiding doesn't last for long because I know how safe it is to show up to my first love with my full self.

In the story of Hosea and Gomer, Hosea is told to marry a woman that he knows from the jump will be unfaithful. Gomer runs off, chases unkind and unfulfilling lovers, and Hosea comes after her. He buys her back; he brings her into the wilderness to love her back into himself. It's a picture of what God does for His people, and it's exactly what He has done, and continues to do, for me. He buys me back. He chases me. He brings me into the wilderness where He and I can have it out, ultimately loving me back into Himself. He loves me with such an intimate love that I know myself more deeply because of who He is for me and to me.

As I've been spending the last 15+ years learning what it means to show up to myself, I'm discovering who God has made Kayla to be. The little girl with impeccable comedic timing has grown into a whole woman that has a quick wit she uses any chance she gets. I've gotten to know the curiosity my Creator gifted me with, and how I can ask so many questions it might make my best friends want to choke me out, but the depth with which I know them and they know me is worth the loving interrogation. I've learned how to harness my skepticism to lead me to deeper intimacy with the Lord, who can handle my doubting and my questioning better than anyone I've ever met.

As I show up to me, I'm learning that I'm pretty great. I'm getting to know someone that longs to have her life marked by her faithfulness: to God, to His people, and to His Kingdom. I want to show up for people the way God has shown up for me.

In learning who I am, and who God is with me, I've un-covered a quality of His that I never would've imagined I could stumble across: His creativity.

It's no secret, whether you've had a conversation with me or you made it this far in this book, that I do not have the life I thought I would have when I was 15. I don't have the husband, the children, or the backyard I just assumed I would have by age 27. When I was younger, I assumed God was gracious and merciful, abounding in steadfast love. Because that's what the Bible told me. I didn't know that He knew me. Like, *really knew* me. My belief about God as a sovereign being over my life had more to do with what happens after I die. I didn't take seriously how Jesus taught us to pray, calling down the beauty of heaven into our daily lives here on earth. In the last few years my vision of God has expanded in the most beautiful way. Yes, He is widely gracious and merciful, abounding in steadfast love. But He is also close and creative.

While I don't have the husband, I have *the actual best* friend-ships. It actually pains me when I come across people that don't know the depth to which they are able to be friends with others. I am not intimately known in a sexual way, but my friends can look me in the eyes and tell something is wrong, often before I'm able to recognize it myself. I know a lot of husbands and wives that don't have that gift.[4] The longing that I have to be known by a husband is met by a creative God that knows what I need more than I even do. He knows it is not good for humans to be alone. And while I'm physically alone the majority of the time, my spirit is not alone. I have deep companionship with my inner circle of friends that al-lows me to be known on a level that I never thought possible. The way God has knit together the story of my life with the stories of those around me is nothing short of creative.

While I don't have children of my own, I have a plethora of kids in my life that I nurture and love and have the privilege of 'parenting' alongside their moms and dads. Not only do I get to steward my influence in the lives of my nephew and niece, I get to

---

4. And I know a lot that do. This isn't a competition. It's a recognition of God's kindness toward me.

be a godmother, I get to be a best adult friend, I get to read books and go on adventures and have conversations about school days over ice cream. I get to mother even though I'm not a mother. And I truly cannot imagine exercising this gift of nurturing any other way in this season of life.

And while I don't have the backyard, I do have patches of dirt that I get to play in because I've been invited into practices of life-giving cultivation (literally) by those that love me. The family and life I thought I would build with a spouse is being built with those I show up to, and who show up with me. Family, I've come to learn, is not just what you're born into but the group of people you decide to become a unit with throughout life. God has seen fit to weave us all together for the sake of His Kingdom and our flourishing.

God is so creative.

And in His creativity He has shown me what it means to come alive to the deepest parts of who I am. He knows that showing up as Kayla, in all of her perceived lack, is often painful and hard. So, He gives me what I need. He gives me the family I want, the friends I need, and the self-awareness to know at the end of the day, He alone is my closest friend, nearer than my next breath.

And as I show up to my next breath, with my friend Jesus, I am confident and secure that funny, curious, skeptical, loving, loyal, brave Kayla will only continue to become more of who she is meant to be as the presence of Christ and His people continue to show up to her.

Epilogue

To Free Beer

"Asking people into my life is not so different from asking them into my apartment. Like my apartment, my interior life is never going to be wholly respectable, cleaned up, and gleaming. But that is where I live. In the certitude of God, I ought to be able to risk issuing the occasional invitation."—Lauren Winner, *Mudhouse Sabbath.*

To the bartender at 4 Hands Brewery in St. Louis that so generously brought me a free draught City Wide in the midst of writing, we thank you.

It's a Sunday night and I'm at 4 Hands, where I've written the majority of these words. LeeAnn called and asked what I was doing, and after I said, "Come meet me, but no pressure, but also come meet me," she let me know that she just wasn't feeling it, so she was going to go home.

Fast forward 10 minutes and I get a text message with a picture from LeeAnn with her standing behind me.

She pulls up a seat, orders a drink, and while we're in mid conversation, my buddy Paul puts 2 4-packs on the bar. I slap the bar top, exclaim his name, and we embrace in a familiar familial hug.

Presence. Showing up.

What was meant to be a typical evening of writing in my favorite environment turned into a couple hours of conversation between people, all three bound together only by the Spirit of God and the willingness to show up and be present.

These words aren't empty platitudes offered for the sake of writing a book. It's my life. All thanks to Sophia Bush and Holy Spirit, showing up has invaded every part of who I am.

These lessons and this life have been hard fought. If I could have learned the principles of showing up without actually having to do it, maybe I would have.

But also.

I am so grateful I have learned how to show up and that I'm unafraid to do so.

So, show up.

Be present and pay attention to how God might surprise you along the way.

Bibliography

"Americans are Single." https://tfoministries.org/single-adult-statistics-in-america

Calhoun, Adele Ahlberg. *Spiritual Disciplines Handbook: Practices That Transform Us Revised and Expanded*. Dowers Grove: Intervarsity, 2015. 174–76

Griffin, Emilie. *Clinging: The Experience of Prayer Third Edition*. Wichita: Eighth Day, 2003. 22–23.

"The Ministry of Presence." https://www.ligonier.org/learn/devotionals/ministry-presence

Nieuwhof, Carey. "5 Reasons People Have Stopped Attending Your Church (Especially Millennials)." https://careynieuwhof.com/5reasonsmillennials/

Powell, Kara, Griffin, Brad, and Crawford, Cheryl. "The Church Sticking Together." *Lifelong Faith Journal* (Spring 2012) 19. https://www.intergenerationalfaith.com/uploads/5/1/6/4/5164069/the_church_sticking_together.pdf

Tennet, Andy, director. *It Takes Two*. Warner Bros., 1995. 1 hr., 41 min.

Terrell, Joe. "Five Real Reasons Young People Are Deconstructing Christianity." https://careynieuwhof.com/five-real-reasons-young-people-are-deconstructing-their-faith/#:~:text=What%20Is%20Deconstruction%20in%20Christianity,different%20perspective%20on%20their%20ofaith.

West, Christopher. *Theology of the Body For Beginners: Rediscovering the Meaning of Life, Love, Sex, and Gender*. North Palm Beach: Wellspring, 2018. 22.

www.ingramcontent.com/pod-product-compliance
Lightning Source LLC
Chambersburg PA
CBHW051725090426
42738CB00010B/2085